CRAWLING OUT C

A WALK THROUGH

JANICE DINVERNO

I know Rick is still watching over me

I dedicate these thoughts and poems to the Love of my Life - my Best Friend - my Rock - my Foundation – My Husband - Rick Dinverno

My darling Rick- you gave me the best years of your life, and made mine Simply the Best. I miss you every day - I only hope to make you proud

ACKNOWLEDGEMENTS

I want to thank my family, my extended family and wonderful friends

My sisters – Patty & Cindy the true meaning of Best Friends

Without you, I would have been lost

Debbie (little sister), Amber & Linda - Thank you for always listening

The whole Bersani family that welcomed me with open arms the moment we met, and continually embraced me in those arms with love and support

Thank you for indulging me time after time with my stories and memories of Ricky. Your loving thoughts and words have been a great support for me. My family, the Bersani's' and my wonderful friends, all of your hugs kept me safe and sound. The love you have shown me has filled some of the gaping hole in my heart; I love and appreciate you all.

I'm not a stranger to heartache and heartbreak, my first Husband Mike died of a rare cancer when we were just 34. My second husband and I divorced after 3 years.

Rick's death was the most devastating event in my life. I witnessed the horrific event, as others tried to save him. I lost my husband, a wonderful man, and a beautiful soul. Rick was the man I was meant to be with the rest of my life. I met him just before my 46th birthday, he was 42, and we felt so blessed to spend the second half of our lives together, who knew that would be only 14 years. As you read the thoughts and poems that poured out me these past four years, you'll get a clear sense of the true loss and sadness I've felt.

We lost ourselves into our own Universe. Somehow, everyone and everything around us disappeared. In that space and time we knew we would become, not just a couple, but, so totally connected and unafraid to step out there and face any truth that presented itself. Being able to say whatever came to mind and knowing it would be received with open arms and mind. We journeyed somewhere that night I'm not sure our minds were aware of all that happened. I felt as if we had been together forever, but the excitement of being new was never going to end. I felt my mind expand, with the revelation and recognition, that this is what I needed and wanted, Rick – he had always been there and the time had finally arrived for us to journey into a place we had never been, but we were so familiar with. We were suspended yet spinning off into someplace, some time, yet unknown to us.

5/24/1997

Rick whispers to me. His words filter through my brain and drift slowly and gently into soft quiet corners of my heart. Lodging themselves permanently into places I can only feel. I remember fragments (I care for you, I cherish you….etc). I only know my heart is so full, yet it will continue to take in all his beautiful words and survive on them forever

The following are some of the cards and notes we wrote to each other.

OUR DECLARATIONS OF LOVE

June 1997- Rick

I saw you before we met - hovering above distant lands

like - some silent seeking breeze – traveling to some silent distant shore

saw you - in mind's eye – traveling lonely like some forgotten pulsing heart

waking with knowing to its' rightful abode

traveling to some forgotten simple place we call our own

3

I'm seeing you - thy shining ways illuminate me

Thy tender touch has found its' way to my Soul only

throughout time - for I only cherish thee

August 1997 - Rick

Thoughts of sparkling dew upon my cheek

Jan, though a thought of you warms my cold and bleak day

Your shimmering eyes cast brilliance upon grey low clouds over me

Brightness ever falls from thy sleeve. Adorn our world always thus.

September 1997 – Jan

Rick – you've captured my heart

Hold it gently – and she beats only for you

Watch her fly and soar with the gladness she feels

Watch her rest in the safety and closeness she now has

October 1997 (yes I fell in love with him - even in this shirt)

4

1997

1998 – Rick

Like some knowing blessed soul

Doors opened – I saw you - Seeing you – I was lost

Losing – I was found

Finding – I awoke

Awake I sang our little simple song

You sang in morning's distant hour

You sang as some singing soaring dove

You awoke – and I was there

My darling Rick

I'm your sun when your day is gloomy

Your sky when you soar

The breeze when you need a lift

Rain when you're parched

Fertilizer when you're hungry

Shade so you won't be scorched

Your light so you never stumble on the path

Everything God and nature has blessed me with

I will share with you as you do for me everyday

Our first Christmas 1997

Yes - I too am standing upon a small precipice

Looking upon this world

I too stand willing to soar

Wings clipped by life's forgotten disappointments

Shall I step out on quivering air

Air I breathe from your mouth

Your air heats up beneath my wings

Furtive long glances - fresh winds surge up

As I look upon thee - your mind soars upon this

Silly little moment - knowing

Knowing – you step upon unseen worlds claim them for your own

Worlds I walked upon

Our engagement - August 1999 Drake hotel in the Tea Room

November 2000 - Jan

Rick – you're the wall that I lean on

The book that I learn from

The pillow that I find rest on

I never will take it for granted

2000 - Rick

My love – I love you my Dinverno

Love – I care for you so much

You – bared naked and cold

Alone – needing me….us

I needing - rejoicing in – want

Aloneness forgotten

Goddess – Master – God Mistress

It's just you – alone –bare

Piling on all those joys – caring – laughter – talking

Sharing within – without doing busy lives

Calm harbor we are

2/2000 – Jan

Ricardo – you bring out a passion in me that will never die.

You've reached into my soul, my heart and my mind.

They all belong to you, you are….

My Love…My Life…My Air, Water, Stars, Moon & Sun

12/2000 – Rick

My beautiful one – you brighten my every day and night

My life is so wonderful with you at the center

I so look forward to our Marriage

Growing and learning with you

My Birthday Party 2001

2001 - Rick

Marriage is –

Like a rock tumbler – as time goes on, edges become smoother

Like building a country – establish traditions

Problem – not partner – is the enemy

Avoid tit-for-tat

Go for new experiences together

Deaf ear to outside critics

Don't take each other/things for granted

Quirks are OK - Seek simple solutions

May 12, 2001- Jan

My Dearest Rick

Only a few hours from now I'll become your wife

Thank you for your calmness the past few days

When I see your smile, and your beautiful eyes,

I know I'll get through the day

Knowing that smile and your handsome face will be with me always

Guiding us - and keeping our love strong

will get me through the rest of our life

5/2001- Jan

Rick – I promise to laugh with you, soothe your fears, support you,

listen to you, talk with you, be your light and keep us on our path

May 12, 2001

Without you, I would be only one shoe,

and then I would hobble sadly thru life

Sox game August 2004

Playa Secreto - Riviera Maya 2008

Cabo San Lucas 2009

Emerald Bay - Mazatlan 2010

Cancun 1/17/2011

1/20/2011 - We're going home today, Rick is alone in a cargo plane, and I'm flying first class. Home now, I meet my sisters & go straight to funeral home. Lots to decide, I'm on auto pilot now there is no time to cry, need to get everything taken care of. The wake is Monday January 24th. Rick is alone at the airport for the night and I won't see him again until Monday. Plans, plans and more plans. Keep busy, pick songs, pick the readings, put pictures together, select his clothes, and make it "perfect".

1/24/2011 - The wake – I don't remember much. Seeing Rick for the first time…he's so handsome. I kiss him, rub his head and chest over and over, talking nonstop to him. So many faces so many words. I won't leave, can't leave his side, I stay by his side all night. Bill and Mark talk about Rick. I say a few words…don't remember much…just seeing all the faces the sadness. Have to go home now, leave him once again…alone lying there.

1/25/2011 - The funeral – It's the last time to hug and kiss Rick. I stand by the coffin, talking to him, how can I go on? Please - can I stay here forever? I give him one final kiss goodbye on the forehead, as Cindy takes me to my seat. Gloria and Patty speak about Rick, we laugh - we cry. The songs I picked are played, Into the Mystic and of course Simply the Best. My last look as we file out…goodbye my darling. Debbie drives me and my sisters to church. Sammie holds me as we walk in. A sea of faces all looking at me, don't let me collapse, I can't fall apart. Armond and Joe give beautiful eulogies. I walk out with the casket, give it three kisses goodbye…he's gone now forever.

The luncheon – All the hugs and kisses, lots of kind words. I'm crashing now, body giving way to the pain, exhaustion, fever setting in, getting sick. I've officially shut down; I sleep for hours at my sisters' house. Days of recovery, home to R&R, back to work February 3rd. Muddle through, one day at a time. Everyone calling, conversations make time pass.

3/13/2011- Today started out the same as every day the past two months. I was groggy, not ready to face the day and reluctant to get out of bed. But I did. Having coffee, I'm watching the horrific news of the Tsunami in Japan. Life really can change in an instant. I need to start writing my thoughts or go crazy.

I went through my memories box, and found all the cards from Rick. I completely lost control, sobbing and barely able to breathe. I'm angry now, fearful and so bored. Rick and I promised to be together forever. We met just 14 years ago, that is not forever in my calendar! My heart hurts so much I sometimes think I'll actually die from a broken heart.

I sit in the kitchen, waiting for you to come in. This was our place to talk, I feel safe here. The silence is so loud. I talk to you every day, but I can't pray for you, that would acknowledge you're dead. Sometimes, I stay up late and fall asleep in my big chair, only because I don't want tomorrow to come without you. I called your phone today, just to hear your voice. The house seems so empty. We filled the house with our love & laughter and even with our quiet moments. Maybe someday this will be a warm space again – maybe if life ever comes back into me.

3/17/2011 - Do you come to me in the night and hold me while I sleep? When a smile crosses my face, have you whispered into my ear? My mind won't stay quiet, yet I can't hear a single thought. I have nervous energy, yet I can't get moving.

3/19/2011 - DEAD… DEAD… DEAD!!! What a horrible word. It even sounds horrible when you say it. It's dull, harsh and difficult for me to say. I also, do not want to admit that you are DEAD. I actually forgot for awhile and thought you were somewhere in the house. The realization comes flooding back as I look around, saying to myself, no, he's not at his desk or in the garage he's gone. DEAD… DEAD… DEAD!!! I scream out to no one. Get it through your head.

3/24/2011 - I keep talking about how quiet the house is. Even in the late hours of the night, while we slept, your presence could be felt. The rhythm of your breathing could be heard. Now, the house it too still, eerie quiet. I have trouble with the quiet; I'm not ready to be alone with my thoughts. TV is my distraction now. My thoughts rush in and ramble on; I can't or won't let them settle to hear my own mind.

3/27/2011 - Today a mass is being said in your name. My sisters and some Bersani cousins are going with me. I'm scared to walk back into that church. Tears are right on the edge. I hear your name spoken out loud in a church filled with strangers, asking all to pray for your soul and for your family, it hits like a bolt of lightning. Two months have passed and the reality is really sinking in.

3/28/2011 - Happy Birthday, My Darling Rick. As I look out at the pond, I watch the ducks and all the birds flitting around, I imagine you as part of it all. You are now my nature – my universe from the shining stars to the budding trees, I see you in it all. As I walk through nature, you'll be by my side. As I look at the Moon & Stars, you'll be looking back at me. Guide me through my days Rick, I'm lost now and can't find the path. I know you're right there guiding me. Why can't I see you? Maybe I'm not yet ready. Are you waiting patiently for me? Do you hear all my questions, my lamenting? You always thought I was strong, am I still. I don't want to be strong. I want to lie still for days, feel sorry for myself, let myself go and not care about the world around me. Yet, something pushes me to get up, shower, dressed. It's so mundane, no purpose. I know it's what I "need" to do. Find a routine and survive.

I sleep wearing your t-shirt, and bury myself under the covers. The warmth of you has left and the house is feeling cold and empty.

4/1/2011 – April fools! No not a joke…you are really gone

4/2/2011 - I eat for sustenance, I sleep when my body grows too tired. My voice has grown silent. I talk to you in the house and when I drive. I miss our discussions; endless and sometimes for no other reason except we loved to talk with each other. We were each other's sounding boards; we got each other thoughts and ideas. So many thoughts in my head now, swirling and never settling, hard to focus on any one thought. Dreams are crazy and flickering, like a silent movie. The frames jump from one thing to the next, leaving me confused and exhausted when I wake.

My brother in law Bill just lost his brother Matt; he could no longer fight his battle with Cancer, another one taken way too soon.

4/6/2011 - Rick was my Champion, he would ruthlessly defend me, never doubting in his belief in me. He stood by my side, bigger than life, ready to take on the world. Words of advice: Don't take the things your husband, wife, significant other talk about as insignificant to you. Their past is their history. It's what molded them into who they've become. Their accomplishments are theirs to be proud of. Whether or not you find the stories interesting or, you might think to yourself "I've heard this before" or "it doesn't matter to me, this is their past". It does, and should matter. In that moment they reveal a part of themselves, they can feel vulnerable. Take every story and every precious moment you share and cherish it. Rick and I tried to do that every day. Now, those moments are gone, but, I'm left with memories & stories of his history. Ricky, if I ever left you feeling insignificant, I'm sorry. Sometimes, in our "too busy" of a day, both of us could be too caught up to pay attention to the other. Eventually, one or the other would realize and make a point of stopping what we were doing and take the moment to hug, kiss and listen. So, take a moment now to tell the loved ones in your life how much they mean to you. And to all my family and friends - I love you all and thanks for being in my life.

4/13/2011 - My depression deepens as days turn over and over. It's Spring now, trees are budding & birds are chirping. I've begun to disengage, pulling back, hard to be sociable. I find it difficult to make small talk. Finding busy work keeps my mind free. I linger at the office, no hurry to get home.

I spent the weekend with Linda & Erin. They ask me questions…how do I feel? How often do I cry? When do the scared feelings come over me? They are both so sad for me and don't want to upset me by talking about Rick. I only want to talk about Rick; I need to talk about him. I keep him alive by telling stories.

I'm at the office and it's happening again, it seems my mind forgets what happened and it all comes crashing down on me. Rick is not home waiting for me, no phone calls in the morning; just to say hi, I love you. No more "you look beautiful my darling" every morning. Waves of dizziness and nausea hit so hard I reel in my seat. Driven back, I close my eyes, let it wash over me take me down and jolt me into reality. I sit still for a moment, afraid to move or open my eyes. I fear actually falling off my chair. I look at all the pictures of Rick that surround me. All smiling and saying "I'm happy", I love you". Never to feel that kiss, hear those words again. Too much now, need to stop. My tears are on the edge, not at the office please. Turn it off, focus on work, make the thoughts go away…for now.

4/16/2011 - Life is blooming all around me while I wallow in the darkness of Death. I don't want to heal, whatever that means. I want to feel the sad & the pain. My thoughts torture me. All the what-ifs and should be run through my mind nonstop. Every space is filled with Rick. Everywhere I turn are reminders of us, our trips, there are mementos in every corner. I can't even throw his toothbrush out and his slippers are still in the same place he left them! What's the rush? Can't just erase him by throwing things out, can't bring him back by keeping everything as is. Ahhh such a dilemma, I'll just ignore it all for now.

I have not unpacked his suitcase yet, it's still in the garage. I can't bring myself to even look at his clothes. My clothes are in the laundry hamper, I can't bear to look at any reminder of that trip.

4/17/2011 - It's going on three months he's gone. They say you go through seven stages of grief. There are days I feel as if I'm still in the first stage, denial and also the second stage anger. I rant and rave, cry and even stomp my feet. Screaming, asking why, and crying out - Please Come Back! The simplest things bring tears to my eyes. The shock of remembering that day still hits me hard. Yes, I realize I still can't say he died or dead. I don't like the words in my head or as I see them here on paper.

I carry the Urn of Rick's ashes up & down the stairs every day. They're near me in everything I do in the house. As I watch TV, the Urn is on the table. I put it on the dresser as I sleep and in the living room, so he can have the beautiful view, as I leave for the day. I know it's there to greet me as I walk into the house. This must sound so weird or strange, but it makes sense to me to have him close to me. It's something tangible to touch, hold and kiss as I talk to him every day. Sometimes I sit on the floor and carry on conversations to it, as if Rick is sitting in front of me.

4/21/2011 - A beautiful clear night and a sunny morning, one has to wonder how Mother Nature can be so happy & beautiful while mourning someone who loved her. The dreary days seem to carry the heavy feeling of grief I feel, that I'm ashamed to smile at sapphire blue skies or the hint of Spring in the air. Should this sadness go on forever? Rick loved warm sunny days, I'm sure he wants me to appreciate the changing days.

The weather is turning much warmer and the days following Rick's death are now many. I wondered yesterday: how can the Universe leave behind the ugly, mean, killing humans? How can it justify taking someone with such a big heart, loving nature and a mind created to help the world? Again, I ask, will I ever have the answers? Will I, when it's my time, find Rick and know what really happened to him?

4/23/2011 - I took a short walk through the neighborhood, I cried all the way. As soon as I got to the corner, memories of Rick & I walking together rushed through me. I found it hard to breathe, but pushed on and walked our usual route. We would make comments on the lawns and gardens, holding hands and chatting away. The fear of walking alone hit me and I asked Ricky to please hold my hand. I've walked a couple of 'our' spots, been hard to get through. I need to move through my life now; I'm hoping the next steps will come easier. Funny, how such a simple act can bring up so much emotion. One more step in recovering, next should be easier.

I took another walk along the river, this time I carried your picture with me. We loved walking along the river together. I just kept talking as I walked and knew you were right beside me. It was easier this time and fewer tears, mostly wistful thoughts of us here enjoying nature.

4/27/2011 - It's OK to eat ice cream with whipped cream (even out of the container) It's OK to not want to talk to people, to withdraw. It's OK and necessary to feel the pain, to yell & cry. As I move forward, day by day, there will be sharp turns and blocks in my way. If I speed too much to get through the suffering, I'll crash into a wall. Take my time...feel the anger, be afraid, & stay strong. Talk to Ricky, he's behind you, beside you, guiding you. As you follow you path, watch your step. If you stumble, it's OK to cry & sit for awhile. Then, take a step back, take a moment to assess then walk on through it. Walls are only as high as you build them. Climb on over!

4/30/2011 - There were songs, when we first met, that meant so much to us. The Best of course was our wedding entrance song. I remember how we would hear songs, then come home and sing the lyrics to each other. I keep hearing some of 'our' songs the last couple of weeks. One of those songs was The Reason. The words had so much meaning – "I found a reason for me to change who I used to be. A reason to start new...and the reason is you. I found a reason to show a side of me you didn't know. A reason for all that I do and the reason is you". The words are very powerful. Both Rick and I had a reason to change when we met. I was broken and on the mend. I had a difficult time trusting and opening myself without the fear of being hurt. Rick had his own walls with doubts and fears. I picked it as our anthem, we broke free of our own fears and let go. We welcomed each other and realized we could show each other all of ourselves and be safe.

5/1/2011 - I was remembering 10 years ago; we were drinking a bottle of wine and practicing our entrance dance for the reception. It started out one night, just us goofing around, and then we thought what the hell. Those very late night, wine induced practices with you timing us with saying over and over "truck....truck....truck...stop...turn'...etc. what a riot that was. And we did wow the crowd; people still say how much fun that was.

I sat outside for awhile and looked through pictures. I wander around the house, not sure what to do next. I'm a lost Bunny that needs her Big Dog to shepherd her. I liked having structure. We both did our own thing on the weekends then spent time together. Now, I sit and stare out the window unable to move, just frozen in time. I pretend you're sitting on the couch as I open mail & read magazines. I talk to you like we normally would on Saturday and Sunday mornings. I even answer me in my head as to what you would say when I would ask questions or comment. 'Yes my Darling...I love you my Darling'.

5/4/2011 - As I'm driving home from work, my eyes again well up with tears. This happens just about every night. The thought of coming home to an empty house overwhelms me with sadness. I have a thought; if I could be certain that Rick and I would meet in eternity, and be together forever, I would die now. I know my family and friends would miss me, but I belong with Ricky. This sounds like crazy nonsense as I'm writing, but I miss him so much, that I would do anything, make any bargain to be with him again. I'll sleep on that thought; hope I see Rick in my dreams. Good night my Love.

5/5/2011 - Dull aching pain, as my heart thuds in my chest. I hold the Urn in my arms and press it to my body. Can you feel my beating heart? I wish it would pump life back into you. Can you feel my kisses? Do you taste my tears as they run down my cheeks, leaving a trail on the Urn? Do you hear my plea for you to come back? Is your heart aching for me too? Are you watching over your 'Bunny' wishing you could hold me, comfort me?

5/7/2011 - We thought we were so blessed by the Universe, the Universe loved us. Mother Nature looked after us, always giving us perfect weather for our trips and planned days. We always joked about Mother Nature giving us special treatment because we loved and appreciated her so much. What a cruel joke the Universe has played on us, she took the one person that loved her the most. Since Rick's been gone, we've had record blizzards, earthquakes, tsunami, tornadoes, etc. Maybe the Universe realizes what a mistake it made, and now it takes its anger out on everyone else. Are my feelings of despair, sorrow and anger so strong, too strong to be contained? What you put out to the Universe you get back tenfold? How full of myself am I to believe I could have that power.

I always believed it was fate, karma that brought Rick and I together. What happened that we had to be torn apart? We were both ready to meet each other, it was meant to be. What did we do to lose that? We had big plans to celebrate this year, our 10th wedding anniversary and my 60th birthday. We did celebrate our love and life every day, never missing I love you, a kiss and a hug. This is a milestone year, yet, nothing matters now. I think about us, our life together, short as it was. So much more for us to do and experience, nothing is the same without you here.

The house looks like a tornado came through, papers & mail everywhere. I can't concentrate on organizing anything. I know you'd go crazy seeing all this stuff spread out on the countertop, table and even some chairs! Nothing is important to me right now, plus I JUST DON'T CARE. I can't even get a grocery list together, my mind wanders constantly. Even my writing is all over the place, one thought quickly gets replaced by another. At least it's all being written down and hopefully helps to clear my mind. I've been trying to have breakfast for about an hour. My mind wanders to something and I forget that I'm starving until the rumble starts in my stomach loud enough to replace the thoughts in my head.

5/8/2011 - The days are finally starting to warm up, yet the house feels so cold. I walk around with a sweatshirt and my robe on. All the life has left the house; it feels like my tomb, cold and sterile. My body seems to grow weaker and more tired as days to go by. The sun is shining there are blue skies and birds are chirping; I keep the curtains closed. I want to look, enjoy and feel the sun and warmth but I feel it is a betrayal to Rick to enjoy life.

I was out running errands and I could feel my body shaking, the tears were right on the edge. I stopped at Dr. Toms' office to see anybody, just to get a hug. All the staff was there and just having that physical contact for the moment helped. There's so much I miss about Rick. The touching or lack of it now is the hardest part. We would walk past each other, a simple touch on the arm, a pinch on the butt or a stroke across the head these are constant reminders to us of being alive, being in love, and that we were here for each other. The words I love you darling were spoken with sincerity. I speak these words now to an empty house, putting them out there to the universe to Rick's spirit.

I'm bored I feel my mind going to mush. I can't stand the quiet it's almost painful. If I sit in the quiet my mind goes crazy remembering that day and realizing Rick is not here. So, no quiet for me TV is always on.

5/10/2011 - The calls to check in on me have stopped. Everyone has moved on to continue with their lives. I'm stuck here. I can't fault them, life goes on. They all meant well in the first few months. I'm sure it's hard to talk with me; they can hear and feel my pain and don't know what to say. Clichés have all been said and best wishes sent. I don't think they want to hear how sad I am how often I cry and that I can't sleep. They want to fix me or hope I'm fixing myself, sorry not happening. Sounds whiny I know, I have a right to feel sorry for myself, to be angry, hurt and pissed off. I'm left alone and I hate being alone. I don't want to be angry with you I'm not sure what I'm feeling right now, but it feels like I'm angry with you Rick.

About eight months ago I woke up feeling like you were gone. My heart was heavy and my tears started to flow. For a few days I walked around with this feeling of doom. Finally, I told you my fear of losing you. We talked, I cried, and you promised you'd be here until we were 99. We're growing old together. You should have never promised me! You know how I am once I think something is going to be a certain way my disappointment runs deep if it doesn't go the way I thought. This is disappointment to the grandest scale. As much as I lived the each day as it comes theory. I planned each day to happen with you forever.

Each night before going to bed my heart starts to pound. The palpitations make me visibly weak. The sound in my head is like a muted engine. I hate going to bed alone, I always ask you to come lie with me. The fear settles in, I want you to hold me, rub my head and help me go to sleep. The trembling starts, the bed is cold, you did not warm my side. I face another silent night, no goodnight, no kiss. Again I hold the Urn in my arms trying to remember what your body felt like and the smell of your skin. I kiss you goodnight and place you back on the table. I imagine you're here as I hold the pillow to me. Tears fall slowly down my cheek and nose. Comfort me now, your Bunny needs to rest.

5/12/2011 - Happy 10th Wedding Anniversary to my Love. I'm missing Rick more than ever. We should be celebrating our love our marriage today. Rick was the proudest husband. He bragged about being a bachelor in two millenniums. Then finding me and deciding I was THE ONE. I miss you Rick, sending out love and kisses.

I have mixed emotions today. A ray of sunshine is streaming into my life. A baby, my niece Erin had a baby girl yesterday – Annabelle Wren (Annie), a very happy distraction.

5/13/2011 - I had dinner with Patty and we talked about how I never had a chance to grieve with my family. I spent three days in Mexico grieving alone. Even though Rick's brother and sister in law arrive to help me plan to get Rick home, I was alone. I could not show that much emotion to them, I would cry alone, anguish in our room. Pace the floor and yell at the ocean from the balcony all alone, no one there to hold me or comfort me. They tried; I would share some thoughts never comfortable enough to let it all come out. By the time I get home, three nights later, I was on auto drive. While making funeral arrangements there were brief moments of tears with my family, we had all grieved alone for three days. I wanted to break down and let it all out but never had the chance. When Patty and Bill and I went out to dinner we got news that Bills friend had just passed away. They both left me to go to his friends' house and I went to Cindy's house. I just couldn't bring myself to lay out my feelings to her; I decided she could not handle it… (unfair?) so I talked lightly and cried very little. By the time Patty & Bill came back to get me they were both so sad we just rode in silence. A call comes from my nephew Billy that one of his friends also just died. All the talk now turns to Bill and Billy and how horrible it is to lose a friend. What about me?! My story is now forgotten. Bill's crying, Billy cries, and I'm a consoling both of them I stay strong and don't want to add to their sorrows. Over the next few days planning for all 3 wakes there are some stories shared of Rick and not many tears in front of them. I think it's time to talk with my sisters and let it all out. Somehow I stayed strong never broke down and now many days have passed. I go home to an empty house and I break down. I think my sisters believe I'm OK. I tell them of my moments but they never get to see or experience any with me, it's time

5/15/2011 - I could not find Rick's wedding ring. We had hidden our rings before we left for vacation. He was a very good hider and I've made myself crazy looking for it. I tore apart every drawer, the cabinets, even went through his car. I got so upset; I accused Rick of keeping me from finding it because he was mad at me. I sat here again today crying and asking him where it was. I'm angry that you're not showing it to me, are you keeping it from me. I need it, it was our 10th anniversary, I should have it, and it's the symbol of our love! How could I not find the ring?? Are you mad at me for not saving you life?! I'm crying and pacing, and suddenly I'm back looking in his sock drawer. As I'm saying out loud, I've already looked here; how many times can I look for it! My heart skips a beat as I feel it tucked into the toe of a sock. I was so happy I just sat and cried. Thank you, thank you, today was the day you wanted me to find it. I'm sorry for accusing you of being mad at me. Then it hit me, if I have the ring Rick is no longer wearing it and he's really gone.

I talk about not being able to save Rick's life. I refused to go into the water with him that day. He had his hopes up, I'd taken off my glasses and he said to me "that's it you're going in now". Once we get down to the water I balked, I said the water look too rough for me. I pointed down the beach and said it looks calm down there, why don't we go in further down the beach. He looked and saw all the people in the water and said "nope they'll want to be near me or touch me. That was a joke with us, he always said we were important like celebrities and people would want to be around us. We always stayed away from the crowds sat by ourselves and walked further down the beach. Off he went promising we'd go in together later. They're I stood watching from the shore, and moments later I watched in horror as he fell forward and had to be pulled out. My fear of water held me back from running in to help him. Everyone has tried to convince me it did not matter; I could not have saved him. I wasn't there at his side in his moment of need. I wonder if he was scared and if he thought of me as I stood there watching him in his final moments. I feel like I let him down, I know that's not a practical thought, but I can't help the way I feel.

5/16/2011

STILLNESS

A house so still a mind on overdrive - the quiet should be a comfort

One seeks quite to relax, regroup - this quiet is deafening, pounding

The memories stream by in moments

The thoughts are like a flickering old time movie

Hard to focus on - yet catching small glimpses

A smile here, beautiful brown eyes, glinting with mischief, there

A hand reaching out to me, then gone

A muffled voice, is it you? My imagination making it so?

Calling my name, teasing, laughing

I love you darling... Gone now

The quiet rushes in, loud, blocking all sound

Try to remember... I see you now

That day comes back to me. Your small wave to me from the water

I see you so clear... why that? Why now?

You're leaving me now - the angels are there

They comfort me – then, they take you away

The quiet is broken by my screams... Then only silence

It feels so weird for me today. I feel like I can move to the next step, whatever that is. I've been on hold, hoping to find his ring, unable to finish moving things around or put anything away. I was afraid and feared overlooking the ring and losing it forever. Finding the ring filled me with mixed emotions. I'm happy to have it, knowing it's not lost or thrown out but the reason I now have it is a burden to bear. I put it on a chain and it feels heavy against my skin. The weight of the ring reminds me of who it belongs to and why I now wear it, yet, I feel comforted somehow.

SLEEP

Do you watch me as I'm sleeping   do you gently call my name

Are you saddened by my crying   will you touch me just the same

Do you come to me as I'm dreaming   do you soothe my aching head

As my tears soak into my pillow   will you lie with me in our bed

Will I often dream about you   and that smile that I love

My heart is filled with sorrow   as the early morning breaks

I'll look for you tomorrow   as I sleep and dream again

5/19/2011 - Four months ago I was in Cancun packing up our suitcases to head home. You were in a casket waiting to be sent to the Airport. We were not flying together or arriving in Chicago together. I would not leave Mexico until I knew for sure what flight you were on. We both left Cancun on January 20. I was being well taken care of I had a full breakfast and then lunch at the Airport. As I board my flight I find out I was upgraded to first class, you're in a shipping crate in a cargo hold of a Delta flight. I was home in a few hours, picked up and taken to see my family. You were flown to Atlanta with a 5 hour layover and arrived at O'Hare Airport around 11:00 PM that night. The Airport was closed and you spent the night in the terminal. I was told that there were guards there that night as I slept in a comfy bed.

The funeral home picked you up in the morning as I went home to pick out your clothes for the wake. 48 hours had passed and you spent the next two days alone at the funeral home until I arrived for the wake. It was Monday, January 24, and the first time I had seen you since Tuesday the 18th. The last time I saw you we were in a Cancun funeral home. They had prepared your body and selected the casket for you. About 11pm the priest read the last rites. I was surrounded by Kitty and Armond my friend Gino (who lives part time in Cancun) the funeral director and the four people I have spent the last 13 hours with Olga, Alfredo, Filipe and Pablo. There was a short prayer service and they all read from the bible as the priest blessed you and the casket. We all left you then, and I went back to the hotel for pizza and beer. We toasted to you and talked for awhile as you were alone at the funeral home. I went back to our room alone for the first time that day and sat and cried for you. There was a full Moon that night, and I screamed at the sky and ocean, filled with anger that you were taken from me. I can only think of you all alone and praying that you weren't scared - I was terrified.

Four months have seemed like a lifetime. My mind keeps going back to the day you died, and the days following. I can't even begin to imagine what lies ahead. Right now I don't want to let go of remembering those few days. How did this happen? This is surely a horrible nightmare, a silent nightmare. Mine is the only voice and mine are the only thoughts. Yours have been silenced. I've been sentenced to live on in silence, never to hear your voice again.

5/21/2011 - I'm sipping my coffee staring out at the pond, I thought I heard you, a muffled sound yet distinct. It sounded like you at your desk. Of course it's not, how could that be? My mind plays tricks on me. There are brief seconds, moments that pass quickly that I'll think of telling you something. And just as quickly I realize you're not here. There's not a day that passes without a moment like that. Something happens at work, a song that reminds me of us, so many things to tell you to share with you. That was our life, sharing our moments our thoughts. I just want to call you and say hi and ask how your day is. I do talk to you every day, sometimes it feels silly.

I say goodbye, and tell you what I'm doing that day. I come home and greet you as always, Hi honey I'm home! No response, emptiness, quiet. I keep putting up pictures of you at home and work, Reminders, memories, snapshots of moments in our life. As I look at each one, I remember exactly what we were doing. Never to have that experience again with no chance of new experiences, we are now frozen in time.

The weather mirrors my mood; cloudy dreary and rainy. Or, is it your mood??

When two people are as close as we were it's as if they are tethered together. Now that you're gone it's as if I'm floating in space. We secured each other, grounded each other, without the other we're just drifting through time.

5/22/2011 - I tried to lie on the floor in the space where you always laid. I try to imagine you telling your Bunny to come hug you and lay down with you with you. I felt the impressions in the carpet. I try to remember lying with you as you held me so tight. There was no warmth, no big chest for my head just a hard floor. I cried for you - I cry for me

5/24/2011 - I've decided to see a therapist. Dr. Tom had recommended that I talk with someone. Today was my first meeting with Quinn. We talked about Rick, his personality and our relationship. He then asked if I could tell him what happened that day. I was reliving it all over again. I let my guard down, told the story and let the emotions come. I had not cried in front of anyone like that, it was a great release. This was a good decision. I'm not looking to 'get fixed'. I need a platform to stand on, feel comfortable and let all of my thoughts come up and out. This is pain I'll live with forever. I'm learning how to live with it.

It's easier to sit in the pain - than to move forward and make decisions

5/26/2011 - I was looking through some old photos of my mom and dad, some really old stuff. I started thinking about my mom and Rick meeting somewhere in the Universe. You'd really like him mom, the two of you could be dancing together, just be careful he can step on your toes. I talked with my sisters; I need to let them know my pain is still fresh and raw. When I'm home alone, I'm not OK, I hurt, I ache, and I cry.

I was always searching for Rick. Once I found him, my search was over. That's why we held to each other so tightly. We both knew we found what we had looked for so long ago. We no longer needed anything or anyone else. We were now complete, whole and content.

I'm broken again. Pieces of me scattered and I'm unable to put me back together.

It's late and I'm so tired, yet I don't want to go to bed. I want to see Ricky in my dreams, but I don't. My mind races even while I sleep. I think I hear his voice, I wonder if I'm just imagining or wishing it. I can't think straight, I'll go up now, night - night, sleep tight, I Love You.

5/28/2011 - Home alone, I'm left with my thoughts and memories. I want to think and talk about Rick all the time. I have a fear of forgetting him. I don't hear his voice or see his face. I sit with my eyes closed and bring up memories of his smile, his eyes and how he would look at me. I want to be in those moments forever. Days are moving by and life goes on around me. I move through the week as routine guides me throughout the day. At night, alone, I wander room to room. I talk to Rick, just to say hello or sometimes tell him about my day or how I'm feeling. I resist going to bed each night, never looking forward to the next day. I want to stay here in the moment or remembering my days & nights with Rick. He's here in my heart and mind. I fear as each tomorrow comes, my memories will be harder to recall.

5/29/2011 - The fog is so thick I can barely see across the pond, sort of how my mind feels today. Yesterday I went to visit with some old friends with my sisters. Part of the time I enjoyed talking and laughing, but I also felt like I was watching myself from across the room. At the end of the day I was anxious to get home. Being with more than a few people still overwhelms me.

I also do not feel comfortable talking about Rick in a large group. I need to be able to say what's on my mind as I'm thinking of him, and that's not easy for me in front of a room full of people. Besides, they did not know our relationship or much about our marriage. I'm selfish right now and only want to think and talk about Rick and me.

I've been digging through all of Rick's storage boxes and found all of his early writings from the 70's. What a cheat to the world that such a beautiful mind has been lost. He was brilliant and soulful. I also found his poems about us. My heart is aching to hear his words. At least I can go back and read all the cards and notes he wrote to me.

5/31/2011 - I'm sitting at my office desk and the wall start closing in. I have the shakes now, hard to breathe, I want to scream, yell out...no not here in the office. All the pictures are looking at me, I close my eyes...don't look, don't look. His smile, his eyes, please - stop looking! I have to get up, I'm going numb, quick let's get out of here. I'm walking crying and feelings are pushing in on me. I feel like fainting, shutting down. Just walk, make it go away. I'm panicking; missing Rick so much...I'm alone!

6/4/2011 - Life sucks right now. It can be so wonderful one minute then turn and slap you in the next. I had finally become the woman I was meant to be. I was happy, I loved myself, genuine and proud of whom I had become. Rick had been there every step of my growth. What's the point now? Should I become mean and bitter again? My days seem endless; I can't sleep through the night. Weekends are filled with bad TV. I'm bored but I can't move. Sometimes, I just sit in my chair and imagine you sitting across from me. My body aches, yet I feel too lazy and unwilling to start working out again. Ricky was so proud of me; he loved his strong insightful Bunny. I certainly do not feel very strong or insightful; I'm just stuck right now. I can't see what's ahead of me. I can't even imagine where my life is going now. Everyone is so positive I'll be just fine in time; whatever that means.

My birthday is in six weeks, my 60th. Such big plans we had, my birthday party and to celebrate our 10th wedding anniversary. That's why we picked Cancun this year, to save a little money and really celebrate the big events. What irony is that? Quick easy and cheap vacation and now Rick is gone, DEAD. No celebrating – nothing left to celebrate. Of course Ricky wanted to always please me, so planning for the next year was a goal for him. I know I did not cause his death, but I will always wonder…what if. It's hard to think about our plans and not feel some guilt. My sisters and my friends still want to have a birthday party for me. It seems so selfish to think about celebrating me. I'm torn! How can I celebrate anything without Rick? Celebrating I'm alive, I'm 60! Rick will never share or celebrate another moment with me again. Is it wrong, disrespectful? I'm so lost and confused. What do you want me to do Ricky? I need your help, show me the way. Oh God, I miss you so much!!

6/5/2011 - With the warm weather finally here, I'm forced to go through my clothes from vacation. They've been in the laundry basket; I could not bear to look at them as reminders of that trip or what I wore that day. Rick's suitcase is still in the garage along with his backpack. I still can't bear to open it up, not yet.

I went grocery shopping earlier; I still wander the aisles seeing items Rick would love. I don't eat much or eat healthy. When I come home, I still expect to see you sitting at your desk on lying on the couch. I'm still shocked when I suddenly remember the reality…nope you're gone.

Quinn asked me to start using words such as passed away, died and dead. It's too hard to think of you that way. To me, it sounds too permanent; I'll never see you again. My brain knows the truth, but my heart can't bear it yet.

LAZY SUNDAY

A hot lazy Sunday afternoon

Sitting back watching the day slowly slip by

Sun shining, bright blue cloudless skies

Too hot to be out, sit back relax and read a book

Dozing off letting your thoughts slip away - dreamless sleep

The warmth in the house taking over

Wake with a start, pulse quickening heart pounds

Tears stream onto my cheek - Where did you go?

Weren't you just there, smiling in that way of yours?

Sadness takes over once again

6/8/2011 - I know I can take care of myself but I liked you taking care of me. You always listened to me, you heard me, and you got me. You knew exactly what I wanted and needed. I'm on my own and I have to depend on me. That's great! I can't figure out what to do hour to hour. How can I set a course to travel? One step at a time, carry a good flashlight to light my way. You were my light Ricky we lit the way for each other. My faith has been tested and jaded. I don't want to ask for guidance from my guardian angels, I can't trust them right now. Everyone says that they were with me and protected me that day. I do feel like Angels walked with me for those 48 hours, helping me through it all. Maybe it was you Rick. Either way, why didn't they help you, save you, keep you alive? You should be here now, with me. It should be Us together Forever and Ever! We promised, you promised, we pledged it. How could this happen?! I can't hear your voice, or look into those beautiful eyes. The only thing I see is you floating in the water. Too many tears can't focus on the page. I miss you Ricky, I need you here. Hold Me – Love Me.

6/12/2011 - Life seems to catch up to me on Sunday afternoons. It starts out like any other day, just one of seven. It's the one day I'm home alone with nothing to distract me. Out of nowhere I'm stopped in my tracks and reality hits me. I stop for a moment unsure of what I'm feeling, and then the punch in the stomach comes. It still takes me by surprise and my stomach lurches at the thought of Rick being gone. One minute I'm washing my lunch dishes the next I'm sitting down to keep from crumbling and then the tears come.

Rick's passing has left me feeling vulnerable and scared. I'm also bored and angry, what a combination of emotions. I can't see past this moment right here right now. Am I going to say strong and take care of myself and all the responsibilities I've been left with? Deep down I remember my strength. I'm smart and very capable; I just don't want to be that right now. Rick took on so many things around the house. It was easy for me not to worry about bills or cleaning the bathrooms. Rick took care of so many things I probably took it for granted. Who doesn't? You think your spouse will be there until you're both old and gray. We had a live for today attitude. We met late in life and wanted to savor our time, but, we also made long-term plans. We always talked about the future, whether it was the coming weekend or our retirement years. Now, those plans are shattered broken by his passing. We made plans up to the age of 99. Does that mean I have 40 years to wonder what life would have been like without Rick in it?

Would we still be silly and all goofy as we turned 75? Would we still hold hands as we walked? Would he still tell me everyday I'm beautiful? I'll never know. I would like to think the answers are yes to all of the above. It makes me very sad to miss out on it all. Sometimes, I feel angry not so much at Rick but at life in general. How quickly it turns without any warning. So live for today, love yourself. As cliché as it sounds stop and smell the roses, they might not be there tomorrow.

6/14/2011 - After talking with Quinn, I've tried out a few phrases. Such as; Rick passed away or I'm a widow. None seem comfortable to me. Quinn asked the most important question of all "do you see yourself as a widow"? NO! That's the bottom line. I still don't believe Rick has died. I cannot wrap my brain around the facts, even though I was there and saw it all happen.

I've told the story and I've written around what all happened that day. He thinks I need to write down the whole event, start to finish. Every time I see the image of Rick standing in the water, then falling forward, I push it away. Many times the image of him floating just appears in front of me. NO! I cry I don't want to see it. Maybe if I face it and relive it I can start seeing Rick's face in my dreams. Right now, it's too horrible he looks like a zombie; I don't want to see him like that. I just don't want to remember him like that and all the images of him being worked on. This will take courage and stamina to face, and time. It's 11pm why does my brain start to work and think late at night. The rest of me is tired, I'll face it another day. I'm not ready yet.

I finally slept, it was a rough night. A lot of emotional release seems to happen following my visits with Quinn, that's the point I guess. It's as if I'm frozen in time, I'm unable to move forward and unwilling to look back. I know I'll face it, right now I'm afraid. Afraid of what my body and mind will experience. When I have moments like last night, the crying comes on so hard, so powerful it leaves me exhausted. I feel as if my head will explode as the memories come flooding in.

The theme for now seems to be – I just don't care. I feel as if I'm running on empty, no energy and no movement and no will to do anything about it. In my head I imagine all the things I could or should be doing, I just don't care. I'm not motivated to get moving. Yes, I get up, get ready for the day and get myself to work on time. I accomplish my goals for the day, I'm productive. Once I'm home, all I want to do is sit. My mind struggles with my body, telling me to get up, exercise, and try to do something. My aches and pains are creeping back into my body. If I feel pain at least I feel something. Part of me just wants to go numb, not face what happened. It all seems to be more difficult for me lately. I want to stay still, but life moves on with or without me. I know I'll eventually catch up, but right now I don't care.

6/19/2011 - I was at a small party at my sisters' and I met up with a woman who lost her husband days after Rick died. We talk for a few minutes, sharing our common connection. Amongst the laughter & joking, we agree life just sucks right now. I could see myself through her. Making small talk and a few jokes, but the pain in her eyes is evident. Is that how I appear to the world? She keeps close to the friend she came with as I keep close to my sisters. Our life rafts. Few people ask about our husbands, no one really talks about them. We, as loving wives, bring up their names in a story we want to share. Otherwise they're not mentioned, not here not tonight. I would rather spend time with people who knew and loved Rick. We can share stories, laugh and cry together. He died, but he will not be forgotten.

I sometimes observe how couples are together. The lack of respect is the first thing I notice. There is disregard for each other's thoughts & ideas. It took losing what I had to really see what others have been missing. I feel sad for them, but mostly for me. I had the love and respect I always deserved. I also learned to trust and give that love and respect back to Rick. I mourn for that, yearn for it. My heart was so full; I had so much to give to Rick. He filled my life with pure Love & Joy. With his passing, there's a huge void. I tell him every day all day how much I love him and always will. I had finally opened myself to trust again, to let go and put myself into someone's hands to guide me on the journey of life, a wonderful moment in the fate of time. It was 'meant to be' I always said. Fate, the universe brought us together, made us whole, one complete entity. His heart my heart, his soul my soul. In that same twist of fate the universe, in all that power, took Rick. My life left empty now, only the memory burns deep inside of me. I have to hold onto that or I will sink into the depths of darkness without it. My love will turn to hatred, my hopes to despair, and my faith to disbelief. I feel my mind go blank and anger creeps in. Thoughts turn dark and ugly. What's the point of life now? I dig deep into the memories and I'm thankful for the time I had with Rick. How special those moments are. Yes, life does suck for me right now and probably will for quite some time. One day at a time they say.

I still go through our 'normal' routine when I go to bed. Rick would rub my head and I would place the back of my hand against his chest. I wanted to feel him next to me. Now, I have a big pillow that I pull over and rub the back of my hand across it pretending its Rick's chest. I rub my forehead or the side of my head just as he would, to help me relax and go to sleep. Night night – sleep tight - see you in the morning.

6/21/2011 - First day of summer, five months have gone by. Today's hot and muggy and there are the storms coming tonight. The sirens go off, where's my Big Dog when I need him? I love the storms but they do scare me. When it would thunder and lightning we would turn off the lights and lie on the floor and watch the light show. Rick would hold me when it thundered, saying ooh Bunny that was a good one. Even something as simple as facing a rainstorm, I have to learn on how to check the house. Just one more thing I took for granted, Rick always kept us safe and sound. It's so late I need to get to bed, come on honey hold me and rub my head and help me sleep.

6/22/2011 - It's amazing how much power a simple hug has, especially when you don't expect it or from the person who give it to you. We had a company outing today on the Mystic a boat on Lake Michigan. I was having a nostalgic moment, alone standing at the rail and over walks a coworker, Ambers husband Jason. I was on the verge of tears and he throws an arm around my shoulder and asks if I'm OK, he says 'I can see you're having a moment do you want company or is it an alone moment. With that he hugs my shoulder and kissed the top of my head. Of course that brought the tears to my eyes anyway, but it was such a sweet and genuine gesture and it really touched my heart. Some people try to force me into having a good time, pulling me into conversations. Others let me move at my own pace, they all mean well I guess. This is something I'll figure out with each passing day.

That hug also reminded me of how much I miss hugs from Rick. Human touch, we're born needing it. I made it through the rest of the cruise with a few more moments of thinking about Rick and me in the city, how much we loved it and the lake front. All the memories rushed in and I was saddened at one more thing I won't be sharing with Rick again.

Someone told me that I looked good, had pep to my step and that I looked more alive. That was one of my good days I guess. I do feel smiles come a little easier and a laugh might come out quicker. Yes, those are my good moments. Mostly I see a tired, lost woman. When I look in the mirror I seem to have aged, taken on a few more lines and creases. I see fear in my eyes and the never ending question of why and what now is written all over my face.

6/26/2011 - Another Sunday, it's early and I feel the loneliness creeping in and that scared feeling in the pit of my stomach keeps punching its way out. I still feel like this is a nightmare, that I'll eventually wake up and we'll be back at January 1st planning our trip. It's been almost six months and I still can't think of Rick as 'passed away'. I go through many of our routines and still talk to him. I can hear him commenting or directing me as I do things around the house. I climb a ladder and I hear him 'Bunny be careful, why don't you have shoes on?' and, I answer back… I know, I'm OK as I step down and put on my shoes. Am I becoming the crazy neighbor lady?? I tell him where I'm going, what I'm making for dinner, what the neighbors are doing and I hear him, in my head, answering me back. Is it my way of keeping him alive, or is it my way of denying he died? I don't know how else to go through the day, he's the first one I say good morning to and the last one I say goodnight to.

I feel so lost and struggling to find my way. I feel as if I was blindfolded, taken away, dropped in a deserted area and left to find my way. Without any directions and not knowing where I am, I don't know which way to turn or how to even start. Nothing looks familiar, no landmarks, and no signs to point me in the right direction. So here I sit unable to move, afraid to take a step. Which way do I go? How do I find my way home, what kind of neighborhood is this? Will the people help or hurt me? If I ask for directions, will I be sent the wrong way? Who do I trust now?! Who's going to print out and give me directions I need to follow? I can't even trust myself. I was horrible at directing my life; I was so lost until I found Rick. He became my light and guided my path. Now my world is dark, lonely and scary again. Rick always saw a strength and power in me. I always felt it when we were

38

together; our energy ran off each other. Now, it's like an engine with no fuel to keep it going. Without being started and running on full power, it will slowly rust out and all the moving parts will come to a halt and be rendered useless. I need to find my fuel and keep that engine running. Rick and I built it together and it would be a shame to let it die because he's gone. It's a work of art, a labor of love; we worked on it together building something beautiful. The world still needs to see it, feel it and realize the power of true love. Ricky deserves that honor and I deserve to power on.

6/27/2011 - I have always been a control freak. When I met Rick it took me awhile but I let go and gave up most of my control. It became easier to have Rick take over some of the chores, errands and even some of the cooking. I depended and counted on him for so many things.

I had no control over what happened to Rick in the water and I gave over control to all on the beach that day. I had no choice but to let those trying to save Ricky do what they needed to do. And for a while I was also being taken care of. Very quickly I was thrown into making decisions on my own. I made all the choices, the funeral homes, both in Mexico and here at home, the service, the songs, flowers and prayers. I did it all with very little help except for my sisters and Bill. Over the past months, I've stopped asking for any help. Life ahead scares me and I feel that need to control rising up again. My birthday is in a few weeks, and we're having a small party at my house. Long story short I just wanted a small group, pizzas, BYOB, something simple just to get together to celebrate. The plans have now been taken over and I've been told to step back and let them take charge. I got angry and even cried; I don't feel comfortable having people doing this for me. I miss Rick so much right now he was my voice of reason. We would talk this out and in the end I would feel better and be confident in my thoughts and feelings. Rick was going to throw me this party and we would've planned it all together, now I'm being asked to trust and rely on other people. It doesn't matter that its family or friends it's a huge deal for me. I know everyone means well and there's going to be a party that's what I want. I'm alive I'm turning 60 and that is worth celebrating. There's also a bit of guilt. Rick's gone and I'm worrying or even excited about this party. How wrong is that? Everyone says Rick would want you to be happy. Happy is not how I want to feel or be described. I will smile - I will enjoy and even have some fun. Happy…. not so much.

6/28/2011 - I always talked to my guardian angels, the universe and God - always asked for help and guidance and I'm asking for help again today. I feel as if I'm in a dark room with a very dim a light bulb. I'm afraid of the dark and I just sit there and not move, just like it did when my sisters would turn the basement lights off on me. I'm asking for guidance to my path. If you would light a few candles, so I can see a direction, I'll at least know which way to start moving. It's time to open my eyes and see what's in front of me. It could be scary or even horrible, little glimpses at a time. It's time to see what happened to Rick. I'm not sure if I'm ready to see everything, but at least stop sitting with my eyes closed. As I am writing this, my pulse has quickened my heart is pounding and I started to shake. The reality seems to be closing in on me and I'm going into my runaway mode. That's enough to think about now, need to distract my thoughts just for awhile. It's like saying you're already to go on that monster water slide, but once you climbed to the top you can't even look over the edge and you freeze in place and refuse to take the ride.

6/30/2011 - I lie on the floor, and feel the cold air blowing in. I feel you next to me, your body warm and comforting. We marvel at how beautiful the night is. I wake up and realize it was just a dream. Now I face the nightmare of sleeping alone.

7/1/2011 - I've walked through the days with unseeing eyes and unhearing ears. I woke today to the sound of birds and saw blue skies. Long gone are the days of the blizzards sleeting rains and flooding ponds. Summer has arrived. Maybe the heat of summer will warm this cold lonely house.

7/4/2011 - It's 4th of July weekend the official start of summer. Rick and I would BBQ, head to the lake or go for a walk along the river. Thank God for my sisters! I spent a couple days hanging with them.

I had to ask my neighbor for help, the battery in my car died. Asking for help leaves me feeling vulnerable and obligated. I sat with her until her boyfriend came home and he got my car started. They asked me to join them for the day and I declined politely. They're a rowdy group and I not ready for that. Without Rick here, every time I'm try to sit outside, they keep asking me to come over; I feel I'm a prisoner in my own backyard. I just need time and space for peace and quiet.

I'm a lost the little girl living alone not knowing what to do first or which way to turn. I feel the house is in chaos nothing seems organized or in its place. I don't even know what in its place means. I move through the rooms to pick up clutter, the house is clean I just have a clutter of papers and photos that I pick up and move to another place. Rick was methodical at putting things away; his desk was free of clutter. I'm just the opposite; dishes are clean but I leave them in the sink I just keep using the same ones over and over. Laundry is done, then it just hangs in the laundry room, bills are paid and left on the table. I'm organized at work but I just can't seem to get it together here at home, Ricky was the director of organization.

Ricky if you can hear me, see me, please walk beside me hold my hand... I'm afraid. Afraid to move do things on my own. I don't want to remember how to take care of me.... I want you.

Everywhere I went this weekend I would see couples, mostly elderly, holding hands, playfully teasing each other and some just quietly walking together. I smiled but mostly I was sad. That should be Rick and I years from now. How quickly life turns from fabulous to sucks. I was happy, fulfilled, I loved my life now it sucks that I'm alone.

It sucks I have to support myself - it sucks I have to take care of the house - it sucks I have to take care of the rentals - it sucks I have no one to talk with - it sucks I have no one here to enjoy food with - it sucks I have no one to do things with - it sucks I have no one to be spontaneous with - it sucks I have no one to make love with - it sucks I have no one to enjoy quiet moments with - it sucks that I'm eating ice cream alone

I went up our spot on the bridge tonight to watch the fireworks it just wasn't as exciting, one more thing I'm left to do alone.

7/5/2011 - I still stop in my tracks as I walk through the house. I'm amazed at how quiet the house is. Rick was not a noisy person; you just knew he was around. As I sit here writing, I swear I hear him at his desk. He's shuffling papers, putting his files away and now coming up the stairs to see me. I turn on the fans and TV to have noise in the house, I hate being in the quiet.

7/7/2011 - I feel numb as if I don't have any feelings right now, as if I'm shutting down. It's not a sign that I'm getting better or healing, I'm just tired and I don't want to think. When I walked in the house tonight, I said out loud 'hi honey I'm home, I'm OK, just sad…sad…sad… sad that you don't answer me'. I cried at my desk today. Images of Rick kept coming into my mind, his smile his eyes our times together. Small glimpses of moments we shared. Tears came and went quickly and I cried again as I drove home. A song pulling up a memory brings a smile than tears. Sad…Sad…Sad…I need a hug

7/8/2011 - Images of Rick rushed in on me. I see him on the beach all those people around him touching him. That was the joke – the irony- we were celebrities, people would want to touch us. That's why he went it the water where he did, the least crowded part of the beach. His last moments are of people pushing on and breathing into him, surrounding him. Although they were trying to save his life he would be horrified at all the hands on him. He would always sanitize his hands and face especially after leaving a party. All

42

those hugs and kisses he would wipe away the germs just to stay healthy. Oh the irony of it all.

7/9/2011

SUMMER

Summer once our favorite season - BBQ and sunbathing

Blue sunny skies turn to clear starlit nights

Hot lazy days and slow nightly walks

Birds woke us in the morning   Frogs bellowed into the night

Sounds of sprinklers lulled us to sleep in our hammocks

Summer - a time to remember a time to reflect

Long days to look at what's been lost

Summer I'm jealous of the pace you move at

So slow so smooth no worries

Summer - once our favorite season

Now my reminder of what is no longer

7/10/2011 - I thought I could go through some of Rick's clothes. I find it very hard to decide what to do with them. I try to sort into two piles of throwaway and give away. I only make it through a small pile of old or stained clothes. It makes me sick to my stomach and I end up putting the rest back into the closet. I keep apologizing to Rick on making decisions on what to toss or giveaway. I can't bear the thought of making him angry even though he was fond of donating; it seems like such a final act.

Somehow, I thought it was time to empty Rick's suitcase; yes it's still packed from our trip. As I start to take out his clothes I hold of each piece to remember him wearing it on vacation. They still have that beach smell to them. As I hold his shirt closes and take a deep breath in, his smell comes rushing back to me. I become hysterical and crying so hard, I'm doubled over and almost brought to my knees. I repeat his name over and over crying and sobbing saying I can't… I can't. I stop from the exhaustion and choking from sobbing so hard. I put everything back in the suitcase and put it in the basement. Again I hear myself saying I'm sorry… I'm sorry, you'll need this…. I'll leave it here. I feel him watching me always with me and I don't want to disrespect him. Getting rid of clothes and shoes should not be this difficult, but I feel as if I'm throwing pieces of Rick away. Maybe it's a way to trick my mind that he's still here, I don't want to believe he's gone - that he died.

7/13/2011 - I spent a couple days with Linda, Erin and baby Annabelle to celebrate my birthday. Annie is nine weeks old, so cute with big brown eyes. As I was holding her today, she was intently looking at me and tears suddenly welled up in my eyes. It was as if Rick was there for a brief moment looking right back at me. A shock went through me as I look at her beautiful face and the moment was gone. I told her she's a little angel that was sent to me.

7/16/2011 - It's my 60th birthday - Happy Birthday to me. I'm having a small party tonight, and I have a lot of nervous energy. My thoughts are filled with Rick and what a great host he was. I've lived quite a life already, two husbands have passed away and I survived a divorce. I was so fortunate to have Rick in my life for 14 years. He brought love and laughter into my world and I will carry him in my heart forever.   I want to enjoy this day and stay in the moment. As I think of Rick my heart aches and I feel the urge to cry, I've already had a few moments and it is only 11:00 AM. Everyone wants me to have fun and celebrate today I know they'll understand if I shed some tears.

The party has started and I can't seem to settle in and relax. It's hard to host a party anytime but tonight I feel pulled in all directions. It's time to light the candles and all eyes are on me. They're singing happy birthday and I feel as if I have a deer in headlights look on my face. Now for my toast – 'thank you all for being here - my family who have become my best friends and my friends who have become my family -thank you for putting together this celebration for my 60th birthday - Ricky would be proud - I'm so fortunate to have you all and my life and for your continuing support - I toast to you all and thank you again. So as the song goes… let's raise our glass…cheers'. Whew!! I got through it.

As I open gifts and cards the emotions start to come up. I start with Sammie's card, it is sweet serious and loving each card pulls up more and more emotions. I picture Rick sitting by my side wisecracking over the sentiments and looking at me with his loving eyes. I wonder what his toast would have been, and what his card would have said. The last card is from my sister Cindy, it is very sentimental - a sister bonding card and she wrote about Rick smiling down on us and making my day. Patty wrote she's glad I'm her big sister and for all the times we were there for each other. Well here come the tears no sobbing, just the kind that come when your heart is tugged at. I see everyone looking and smiling and I hear a few awwws. Sammie breaks the mood by declaring Auntie Cindy's card is the winner, she made Janice cry. We all start to laugh. Overall was a good party. I just kept waiting to hear what Rick has to say. His cousin said the same thing 'he's just in the other room and he'll walk in any minute now'. They all missed him, and each one brought up his name over the course of the night. This is his family, these are his friends too. Rick touched so many lives and we all miss him. The ones that knew Rick the best tried the hardest to make it a fun evening. We did this in Rick's memory and to celebrate that life goes on.

7/21/2011 - Six Months! Six months I haven't had your kisses or your touch. Six months unable to see your face or look into your eyes. Six months not hearing your voice or your footsteps. My body aches for you my heart is broken, my mind hungers for your words. Six months, of no laughter, no lovemaking and no heady conversations. Six months of silent, cold, dreary, boring hell. Six months seems like an eternity. Yet, I have the rest of my life empty ahead of me. My stomach turns at the thought of years without Rick in my life. He filled every corner of my day. Everything looms large and empty now. Our world was ours alone complete small and compact. It was comfy, cozy, and warm and filled with joy love and laughter.

I look at Rick's photos and watch my videos of him, seeing him alive so full of life, his energy filled all space. Such a vibrant personality cannot be snuffed out. I feel him out there I want to hold his hand again feel his strength against my body. Just standing next to him I felt safe and protected. Now I feel small and vulnerable unsure and scared. Don't let me retreat Ricky push me forward and let me feel my power and strength

7/22/2011 - Screams loud and primal coming from inside yet no sound is coming out of me. I can hear them in my head but nothing but a moan a whimper escapes my body. I want to scream and yell it won't come out. Ricky deserves that passion. Tears flow as I cry for him. I call out his name I say I love him and let the tears come. I miss him more and more each day.

7/23/2011 - It was the Osgood family reunion today. Rick embraced my family and they loved him back. His wisecracks and witty conversation always entertained us. My Cousins all hug me and looked me straight in the eye and ask "really - how are you doing"? No tiptoeing allowed in this family, this group is straight up and they want to know the answers. Then, they tease me about turning 60. When someone close to you dies, whether young or old you can't help but look at your own mortality. I looked around the room during the reunion and realized were all old or much older than I remembered. Why, when you're a child, do all the adults seem so old? I found out my aunt is only 24 years older than me. I'm just making an observation that I find interesting.

As I turn off the TV to get ready for bed, I have another one of those odd moments. I stand there for a few seconds, and confusion sets in. I look around for you. It's time to go to bed where are you? Just as quickly the moment passes and I'm looking right at you, right there in front of me, well not you in person but the urn. I just stand there with no thought, no words, just staring. I start to talk to you 'I'm at a loss for words I want to say something but I'm not sure what to say. I just looked for you and here you are here you've been. I'm talking to an urn'. I need to go to bed I don't want to think about this right now, I want to shut down. So what do I do? I decide to write my thoughts down right before I go to sleep. Now I have a pain in my chest my heart feels heavy and whatever is trying to come I'm pushing it down. I can actually feel my body changing. My pulse quickens I can hear the beating in my head my stomach gets jumpy and here come the tears. Quinn said I should not fight the emotions. I tried, I'm tired I did not want to cry it's exhausting and so is trying to hold it back. Those are some kick ass strong feelings. When they're fighting their way out there's no stopping them. Finally, I can say goodnight and hopefully get some sleep.

7/25/2011 - I just had an interesting drive home after my appointment with Quinn. Within a few minutes tears are flowing. I heard a song on the radio by Pink – Who Knew. The words are right on and they hit me hard. *"You took my hand and showed me how you promised me you'd be around I took your words and I believed 'cause you said forever and ever".* That was our saying so many years ago. We would say 'we'll be together forever' and the other would finish the sentence 'and ever'. I'm driving and crying finally a loud moan comes out and I'm banging my hands on the steering wheel. I'm singing and crying along with the song. *"That last kiss I'll cherish until we meet again".* I come to a stop sign and I'm moaning and hitting my head against the headrest. The song is coming to its end *"I keep your memory you visit me in my sleep… who knew"?* It sums up perfectly how I feel and how life can turn so quickly and become ugly. I cried all the way home I guess all the emotions I was pushing down last night were right there and ready to spill. I lived most of my life without Rick and to have him for such a short time it's not fair. I'll never have him in my life again. I carry his memory but I'm afraid of forgetting or losing that memory as I age. Our love was meant to go on forever and ever. Time is moving quickly, life goes on around me. I just want to stay in that last moment of walking on the beach looking for shells. Ricky and I flirting with each other and yes our last kiss. That kiss and saying I love you are my last memories. The next time I kissed him was at the funeral home six days later. I leaned over the casket and kissed him three times which was our routine. This should not be the memory I have to live with. We had our forever and that was 14 years.

7/29/2011 - I was accused the other day, by a long time friend, that I'm not being a very good friend. She said I never really ask about her life. Really??!! In my writings the past 6 months the ongoing theme has been how disconnected I feel from my friends and co-workers. I've had this discussion with her not too long ago and right before my birthday. Of all people, I thought she would understand and see how I struggle. We see each other every day at the office. Now I feel like crap thinking I'm a horrible friend, and does everyone else think the same. I've recognized the fact I have a difficult time carrying on conversations and I've let everyone close to me know about it. UGH! I'm now consumed with this thought of being a "bad friend".

7/30/2011 - Today is Joe and Brenda 25th wedding anniversary party. This is my first large event without Ricky and I'm feeling anxious. All I can think about is how we should have celebrated our anniversary with the same group. I feel the pit in my stomach mostly it's the unknown and I'm not sure how my emotions will be. They will be renewing their vows, I'll be sure to bring lots of tissue. I've already cried a few times today. The ceremony was wonderful and I made it through without many tears. There's lots of love in this group we talked about Rick, everyone had funny stories to share. After dinner we watched a slide show of Joe and Brenda's wedding. A picture of Rick popped up; there he was big as life with that great smile hamming it up for the camera. I think it took a lot of us by surprise and I burst into tears. We all hug each other saying how much we missed him which led to more funny stories and by the nights end we were laughing again. We later watched the video again and there he was looking at the camera with that take your life with gusto look he had. I felt him saying - live life Bunny.

7/31/2011 - After seeing Rick in the video yesterday I decided to watch the slide show we had put together for the wake. I hadn't watched it even though I picked out all the pictures. As the slide show progressed, the shaking started; the tears came and finally a long low moan. I start to cry harder, I'm stamping my feet and yelling out. As the last photo fades to black, it ends with a picture of him gazing out over the ocean, I cry out "no Ricky don't go". I sat and cried until I was choking and couldn't breathe.

I swear there are times I think I'll die from a broken heart. I've been lying around and unwilling or unable to do much of anything. I think about curling up in bed or on the floor and just let my life slip away. Days later, when someone finally finds me, they'll say she just couldn't live without Ricky. But some force keeps me moving, pushing me to eat and sleep. I'm able to laugh and crack jokes but on the inside the pain is real and deep. There's no medicine to take it away and no bandages to cover and heal the wounds. It runs through my body at will and releases through my tears. There's a gaping hole that can't be filled. I can forget for a moment, an hour or even a day, but for now only love and trust will mend it over time. Love from my family and friends and from me loving myself. Trusting that I can take care of me will lead me to believe I can survive, and will live without Rick's physical presence. I want to believe he's around me, that his energy is here comforting and guiding me. There are days my faith in that is tested and I feel small and alone.

8/6/2011 - It's Friday night and I decided to stay home instead of going to my sisters. I ran my usual errands stopping in the usual stores and picking up some of the same foods I would for Rick and me. I even ordered a Lous pizza. The day seemed so ordinary so routine. I remember looking at the clock and thinking, I'd better get home Ricky will be waiting and he'll be hungry. As I pull out of the parking lot I shook my head as if to clear it. Rick is not there! He's not waiting for you! I start crying and hate the fact that I decided to stay home. Then I thought why not make it a 'usual Friday'? I walked in the house said hello to Ricky as usual and told him I was having pizza and salad. I laughed and said it will not be as much fun or as enjoyable without you here. I guess if I'm home on a Friday this will be my new normal I'll just have to make in my own.

8/7/2011 - My sisters, Bill, Nick and I went to my cousin Russ (Squeaky) 70th birthday party. When Russ gave a speech thanking each person by name, it was so weird to hear my name without Rick's. It felt like a mistake as if he forgot to mention him. This was a group that did not know Rick, we only see Russ once a year and he met Rick twice. Several people thought I was divorced and asked if I was out dating. There were a couple of awkward moments because I still don't know how to say Rick has passed away. It seems so difficult to say out loud, especially to strangers.

8/8/2011 - I walked in the house and it struck me again as to how quiet it is. I still come home and yell out - hi honey - out of habit. I want you to know I'm home and safe. It seemed even more quiet than usual, so still and no air moving. It's raining yet I heard nothing as I walked in. I sat in my chair in the living room; I haven't sat there in awhile. I looked across at the couch and tried to imagine you and how you would stretch out and we'd sit and talk for hours. I could not bring up the image and see you in my mind's eye. I started to cry, I'm afraid I'll forget how you looked. I see pictures all around me and I can watch videos of you, but when I close my eyes or stare the couch I have no image. Maybe I'm trying too hard or trying to force it. I want to remember how you looked at me. All your little nuances, a soft smile when you said you love me, a big grin when I walked in the room. That is what I miss the most, you saw me when you looked at me and you talked with me. You saw me as I was and I was as you saw me. I became who I was meant to be, and you loved me for that. You needed me to need you and I needed you to validate me. Together, we were complete

I remember you Ricky

Standing on the corner waiting to meet me - making me feel at ease

Talking with me all through the night - kissing me soft and sweet

Holding my hand and claiming me as yours - Whispering your love to me

Opening new worlds to me - patient and caring

Crying if you thought I was angry - Laughing with me and how silly we were

Vowing your heart and soul to me - making our home our haven

Listening to every word I said - sharing all your thoughts with me

Saying I'm beautiful - smiling when I walked into the room

Always making time for me - Watching stars and meteors with me

Making our world complete -Holding me in your arms

Rubbing my head as I fell asleep - Chasing me around the house

Pinching my butt - biting my neck - Making me laugh until I cried

Never wanting to let go of me

Walking in nature with me enjoying bright sunny days

Walking on the beach   picking shells and rocks

Swimming like a dolphin   being proud of me when I snorkeled

Kissing me at the beach - Saying I love you as you walk into the water

Jumping in the waves   waving to me as you swim

Falling into the water   lying still on the beach

Feeling cold as I held your hand - Dying on a beautiful beach in front of me

All alone covered by towels

Lying in a coffin as I kiss you goodbye

I remember you Ricky - as the love of my life

8/13/2011 - I was moving along the highway of life. Rick and I found the road to travel that was wide open, full of love safety and adventure. We had very few detours or potholes. Our ride was smooth and easy, beautiful sights along the way. Then a dead end appeared a roadblock for me with no turning back. Now my direction has turned me on to a dark scary road. I have no lights no map and no guide. I have to use all my senses to decide when and where to turn. Once again I'm left to find my way alone. For now I'm driving in circles, it's safe but I'll stay in the same place. I feel scattered and pulled in all directions with my family, friends and work. I feel my energy draining on giving all of myself to everyone else. I'm focused on my family right now and that distracts me from my stuff.

8/14/2011 - I loved my alone time on the weekends, especially Sunday, I'd sit out on a warm day and read a book or I'd catch up on recorded TV, maybe go for a walk. For a couple hours, Rick would putter around and I would take this time to relax and recharge. I was reading my book for about an hour, and for a brief moment I thought Rick was standing and watching me. He would do that sometimes, sneak up and just stand there with a smile on his face watching me. A pang of sadness takes my breath away. This is when I miss him the most, when I have quiet moments my mind reminds me I'm alone. I talk to people all week, but I miss my talks with Rick. I used to relish my alone time, now I feel trapped in it. For a brief time I was lost in my book, now I feel restless. I need to escape forget that I'm here alone….always.

I feel agitated and can't wait to get out of here. It's a beautiful day; I would have sat in the yard for hours. We would start in the morning with our coffee and talking, then, we'd both take care of things around the house. We would always end up back in the yard enjoying the sun, listen to the breeze through the trees and usually doze off. I have not sat in our yard, I can't. I tried, but it made me so sad to look at the pond and remember our days out here. This was our little oasis, I feel isolated and vulnerable on our own patio; I sit in the driveway now.

8/16/2011 - It's a bittersweet day, my niece Sammie turned 21. I still think of her as the little girl jumping into my arms.

You came into this world Samantha Claire Hinman

A strong, healthy, beautiful baby girl - you went from being an inquisitive toddler,

to a smart talkative pre-schooler - you excelled at sports from the start

there was no keeping you down. - you had on a baseball glove by the age of three

from floor hockey, basketball, baseball & volleyball

you always did your best and exceeded expectations

I've seen you lying in a hospital bed, brave as can be, being Daddy's little girl

you've melted my heart over all these years a sweet little girl screaming "Auntie Janice"

as you ran and jumped into my arms sitting on my lap, even to this day

all your hugs and "I love you" filling me with Love for you

I've watched you grow-up, always sure of yourself

all the shopping for dresses for the dances Junior Prom, your Prom

and then Graduation I've been there for it all, so proud of you

now, you're a wonderful 21 year old young women,

strong, smart, funny & sensitive

a woman who held my hand when I was scared

who sat with me just so I wouldn't be alone

who nursed me when I was sick, and even gave her bed up for me

and who can make me laugh when I'm sad - you still melt my heart

stay true to yourself and always go after your goals,

you will continue to exceed expectations - I've been there for you through it all, and now

as women, we'll be there for each other - I wish you Love and Happiness

8/21/2011 - It's a beautiful sunny day to day and I decided to take a ride to the river where Rick and I used to walk. I took a small spoonful of his ashes with me. When I pulled up I was second guessing if it was something Rick would want me to do. As I step out of the car a Cormorant, a bird we always see on our pond, flew right over my head. I knew then Rick was there with me and it was OK. I stand by the little lookout and let the ashes float into the water *'Mother Nature I give a gift to you - I release Rick's soul and energy to you to carry on your wings and soar into the universe'.* Then I walked to the bridge we had crossed so many times. I let the ashes drift into the air and be carried out over the water. *'There you go Ricky soar and be free - become part of nature - truly you are now ashes to ashes - dust to dust'.* A hawk floated overhead soaring high and then flew away. I knew Rick's energy was being merged with nature

It is early evening and I decided to sit in the living room in my favorite chair. This is another space I've had a difficult time with. It's just a chair, but it's where I sat every weekend to enjoy my early mornings with Rick. I want to sit and relax and read for awhile, I read about 45 minutes. I lay the book in my lap and close my eyes. The sadness came upon me so fast I didn't have time to think. I started to cry which then turn to sobbing as I kept calling out for Ricky. It was over as quick as it started; the only thought I had was calling his name over and over and then seeing his face floating in the water.

8/24/2011 - It's as if I live in one room. When I come home I change clothes and head right to the kitchen. Once I'm there I move from the table to a corner chair and back to the table. I check emails look at Facebook and watch TV. I'm living in about 4 square feet! Once in awhile I think of going upstairs to sit in the big comfy chair and watch a bigger TV but I just sit right back down. Hey, I don't need to go far for a snack. I feel comfortable here and safe. Once I go upstairs the day is drawing to an end it's almost time for bed and one more day has passed without Rick in it. Each day that goes by takes me further from the last day I spent with him. Or… it brings me one day closer to me dying and hopefully joining him again. Oh! I just heard Rick say "take that back! Don't talk about dying!" The fact is Rick; I'm the one person who never wanted to talk about death now it's all I think about.

8/27/2011 - It's good to see I can now laugh and truly enjoy myself. I spent Friday and Saturday with Erin and baby Annabelle. She's just over three months and a delight to be with. Her smile brightens the dark corners in my brain. My laugh comes easy as she attempts to roll over and at the look on her face. On my way home I stopped at my sisters. Both Patty & Cindy were there and I stayed much too late. It's hard to leave the comfort of family.

8/28/2011 – my niece Sammie is coming over to pick up Rick's car in a couple days. As I was cleaning up the car getting all the papers in order that deep sense of loss started to settle in again. I cried and said goodbye to the car. I know it sounds silly, it just seemed normal to come home and see Rick's car still in the garage. It was as it should be. I would always get that warm feeling in my heart as the garage door went up and I would see his car, I knew he was in the house waiting for me. Even now seeing the car does give me comfort it's as if nothing has changed, now it won't be there to greet me. As I am writing this my heart is aching and there are tears in my eyes. It's another goodbye for me and the first big change around here. Nothing in the house has been moved or changed, I haven't thrown away his toothbrush his slippers are still in the living room and his suitcase is still packed. It just seemed logical to me! Now I'm scared as to how I'll accept seeing the car drive away. I'm thinking about this too much! I'm starting to shake and I feel nauseated. I know it's just an object but it was Rick's for 10 years.

This afternoon I went to West Dundee to walk along the river. I wondered if I would feel different after I had spread your ashes into the river. As I stood on the bridge I asked you to let your energy flow through me. I closed my eyes and all the memories of so many walks came back to me, every path and street we had walked, it was all around me. I can see you kayaking on the river and our eventful canoe trip. As I walked along I imagined you holding my hand, and I admired the blue skies and gentle breezes. I can only hope your spirit is free and your strength is part of the energy around me. There are days I have my doubts and I feel so alone and small. I try to stay true to our beliefs that the universe is our energy. We as bodies are a small speck in the immense universe and we will become part of it all someday. Ricky you know it's hard for me to wait and I want the answers to this right away.

8/31/2011 – As Sammie drove away in Rick's car I was filled with love and pride. She's all grown up but I felt like she's 16 again, driving on her own for the first time. I told her she had to keep the picture of Rick in her car somewhere as he would watch over her. Now it's so weird looking at the empty space in the garage. I know it's a good thing; she will be safe in this car. Let's see how I feel in the morning or when I come home and look at that empty space. I suppose I'll get used to it, just like I am in our bed, I'll start moving to the middle.

9/1/2011 – In my world, I have my own reality. I kiss Rick goodbye and tell him my plans for the day and always say 'I'll see you later'. I kiss him goodnight and say 'I'll see you in the morning'. This is my coping device; I don't want to face it any other way. Some may think I'm kooky or they're uncomfortable with the thought of me saying 'hi honey!' as I walk in the door…I don't care. I keep him alive in my mind.

9/4/2011 – Labor Day weekend signals the end of summer, dark mornings and early sunsets. It's depressing thinking about being housebound again, I just started feeling comfortable going for walks on my own and sitting outside. Time is flying by but missing Ricky has not diminished. I ache for him.

Gloria and Dean are getting married today; Ricky should be here for this. I imagine him there cracking jokes and of course having a speech for Gloria. As I listened to their vows and the minister speaking of love and respect thoughts of our wedding day and our life went through my mind. I managed to hold back the tears. Today is about them and I want to enjoy it and be in the moment. It was a beautiful ceremony and they look so happy. Later we shared stories of Rick and everyone made sure I was OK. I've been permanently adopted into this family.

9/6/2011 – Thoughts of Rick and how he died keep going through my mind. I know I said to trust the autopsy; it's the not knowing for sure that keeps plaguing my thoughts. I'm filled with doubt and replaying the images of Rick in the water over and over in my mind. They're horrible images to watch and remember, but something keeps nagging at me. I'll never know for sure what happened, so why now? All these months gone by and it's all I can think of right now. I was in such shock when I went to the police to give my statement. I told them what I saw and how Rick was acting as he fell forward. I remember saying maybe he choked on water, did I influence the autopsy? I know the outcome would still be the same, people tried to revive him and could not. Rick's death will always be a mystery to me. Our fate was in the hands of strangers in a foreign country. Maybe this is a new guilt for me to deal with; I had put my trust in all these people and did not question the results.

9/12/2011 – I saw Dr Tom today for health coaching and some adjustments. He asked why I'm not out walking like I used to and what else do I do on weekends? I said once I'm home I feel guilty going back out the door. Not sure why that started. I'll go to a social event, and feel guilty. I'll take a day off if I've been busy over the weekend; because I feel guilty I haven't been home with Rick. We talked about my eating and exercise and how I need to figure it all out. That statement just reminded me I'm taking care of me…not Rick & me. It was always Rick and me, why I wanted to look good and eat right. I told him it's as if I just don't care right now, why should I cook or get dressed? I hope I realize some of my thought patterns and I'll start taking better care of myself.

9/12/2011 – I still miss Rick so much and I still talk to him every day. I've noticed there's a little less crying mostly sadness and missing his talks with me. At night I still ask him to come to bed and rub my head and help me sleep. I feel the shift, something different in my days and it scares me that I don't cry for him as often. I want to hold onto that pain I'm not ready to face the world on my own. I wonder if it's because people aren't acting as sympathetic around me and I respond by acting as if I'm OK. I still want to talk about him and I want everyone to feel sad for me. It seems a part of me it starting to accept that Rick is gone.

9/14/2011 – I'm feeling left behind, left out. Everyone seems so busy these days, calls are few and no invites to just hang out. My sisters are there for me, even then I sometimes feel like a third wheel. It's hard for me to ask people to get together. I feel I'm taking up their time or I'm a burden and they don't want to be surrounded by my pain. As I write this it sounds so silly, I'm a Big Girl I know how to talk to my friends. I guess when people see me I look ok on the outside; they have no idea how I'm feeling because I'm self conscious to share. These are my family and friends; I should know they'll accept me as broken right now.

I've been walking more and more along the river, I found it comforts me. Sitting on the patio is still difficult for me. I can't seem to relax out there; I always picture Rick puttering, picking weeds or sunning in his chair. I feel so sad I just can't sit there for long without crying. So the river it is and at least I'm moving.

A WALK

As I walk along the river   Are you there beside me

I feel the breeze gently caress me   Are those your arms around me

I feel the warmth of the sun   Is that your kiss on my neck

The wind rustles the leaves in the trees

Is that you whispering I love you Bunny

The path feels sturdy beneath my feet

Is that you guiding me safely?

The hawk hovers over the water   Is that you watching me

As I walk along the river   A smile comes to my face

Is that you I feel beside me

9/15/2011 – I keep having vivid yet disjointed dreams, nothing that makes sense to me. I saw my first husband Mike, and kept asking why he died. He just hugged me and smiled that huge smile and never answered me. No dreams of Rick yet. I ask him every night to visit me in my sleep and talk to me in my dreams.

9/17/2011 – I'm feeling very confused and pulled in too many directions. I can't seem to settle on one thought long enough to even decide if and where to grocery shop. It's hard enough to take care of me, but now I'm taking care of our house and the rental units. Problems keep popping up with the rentals, one of them needs the shower pan replaced. Finding someone to do the work is taking a lot of research and money. I stood in basement and cried, this is Rick's domain, he had all sorts of project ideas and notes on things he wanted to do. I'm lost; I don't know where to start. UGH, I'll figure it out, I have too.

It's a beautiful day, it's after noon and the last weekend of Summer, and I can't make up my mind where to head out to. I've been trying to leave for an hour, my mind is running wild today and I can't focus. When I'm overwhelmed that leads to eating, which pisses me off which leads to depression and then to chocolate! It's been so long since it was just me taking care of me that I forgot how to do it. Before I met Rick I was a mess I ate fast food, drank and I went out a lot. I was not comfortable on my own; I had only figured that out a few months prior to meeting Rick. The past 14 years have been about the two of us. I don't understand how all the knowledge I gathered about healthy eating seems to be forgotten. I just don't care about me right now. I'm sad, I want to stay sad, and by not taking care of me helps feed that sadness. I know you're asking - if you can write about what you're thinking and you're aware of your thought process the obvious question is why not change your actions?! Like I said, right now I don't care even if I do write about it. It's to get my thoughts down, out of my head and for future reference to look back at when I finally do move forward. I have faith I'll figure it out, I really can't see too far ahead right now. Like I said months ago it is easier to sit in the pain than to make the choice to move forward. It's frustrating to stay in one place but it's scary to take that first step and fly. Hopefully my mother instinct will come up one of these days and push me out of that nest.

I guess I've been saving up some tears. After dinner once again I attempt to sit in my favorite chair in the living room and read my book. I just start talking out loud to Rick and the now familiar pain starts in my heart and the tears flow. The deep sadness sets in and I feel so alone. I ask, how did a beautiful day in paradise go from 'I love you honey, this has been a great trip so far' to 'I'm sorry Mrs. but there is nothing we can do for your husband….he's gone'. How does that happen? All these months later and I still can't believe he's not walking through the door. No more hugs & kisses, no laughter, no words, just a silent house mocking me as I try to relax. Stupid! It's just stupid as Rick would say. I need to hear his voice; I'm going to watch a video of him.

9/20/2011 – the end of summer is upon us which means I'll throw myself into the new TV season. I don't allow myself to think and TV is a good distraction. I can only push the pain and feelings down for so long. It's actually worse if I'm distracted for too long, when the feelings rise up and the realization hits, it hits hard. That sick sinking feeling comes out of nowhere and my stomach lurches like I'm riding a roller-coaster. I cry every time I'm driving home, I think my thoughts catch up to me in the quiet of the car. I put the radio on and it never fails, some song comes on it stirs a memory or brings up thoughts of Rick. This driving home and crying is very dangerous; in a few seconds my eyes are filled with tears and I'm trying to stay in my lane as I wipe my eyes. I still have a hard time sitting in the quiet house. All these months later and I expect Rick to come through the door or to find him waiting for me as I walk in. Some days I'm so disappointed that he does not answer me when I yell out 'hi honey I'm home'. I'll stand in the foyer for a moment really thinking I'll hear his voice and that he'll answer me. I just sigh, put my stuff down, kiss the urn and sit and talk to him for a bit. The fear still creeps up and that feeling in the pit of my stomach makes me dizzy. As I'm walking through the house I scoff at myself saying 'what were you thinking'? You know Rick is not here! There are some days, moments or mornings I simply forget. I don't want to remember, I think my mind likes to pretend nothing has changed. I'll rush home to see him, or when I get up in the morning I'll look for him, I'll just stand there looking around and listening for him. Oh my God! I can't stand listening to the house without Rick in it. How could you have left me? I hate being alone! You were the point to my counterpoint you challenged me and made me think outside of my comfort zone. Now I'm silent and I no longer have a voice. What is there to talk about and why?

In the quiet all I hear is my heart beating, pounding in my head, a cruel reminder that I'm still alive and the sadder I feel, the louder it gets. I hold the urn to my chest like I've done so many nights hoping my beating heart and the warmth of my body can be felt by Rick. I rock back and forth holding him to me so tight I don't want to let go. The urn is hard and cold yet I find some comfort holding onto it. It's all I have left of Rick, he's in there reduced to ashes but there is some consolation that at least I have that. I have something to touch to feel and to hold. It's here in the house with me I see it and I talk to it. I couldn't bear it if Ricky was buried someplace now he's here with me forever and ever.

9/21/2011 – I went to a wake tonight for woman at work whose husband passed away suddenly. I watched her as she greeted guests with a forced smile and glazed eyes. She nods as people talk but she'll never remember what they said. I see the pity and sympathy in all their faces as they hug and kiss her and try to make small talk. Soon she'll be alone lying in their bed, reaching out in the night wondering where he is. She even said to me - it's not real yet I can't think about it now. Is this how I looked to everyone? I can't remember much of that night I only know how lonely I am now. Will she too imagine him there, have conversations with him, and tell him about her day? Do we all, as widows, suffer through our days and cry into our nights? I know my pain and I truly sympathize with hers. Soon she'll return to her life and struggle every day to make it through. The phone calls will stop, coworkers will soon forget and no longer ask how she is and life will go on. I wonder, do they ever think about what goes on behind our closed doors?

9/25/2011

UNDONE

Life too short too fast

Uncertain years - youth of trial and fears

A brilliant mind develops

A leader friends would say

Goes out to conquer his world

Troubled teen shunned

flees to find himself

Streetwise young man - holding out a helping hand

Returns home strong and proud–

Still living his life out loud

Finding love his one desire

A street corner chance encounter

Wedding bells his life now full

Tears of joy heart bursting with the love

Blissful years a partner at last - Shared interests new experiences learned

Yes my darling I love you my darling - His mantra for life

A life filled to the brim - A life too short - so much left undone

MY HUSBAND

So full of energy a bounce to your step

Quick with a joke and laughter - Soft kisses and warm hugs

Proud man with a strong spirit - Giving all of yourself

Always supportive full of encouragement

Selfish of your love only giving to your Bunny

Always putting me first - ready to take on the world

A gentle soul - Loving arms ready to hold tight

A prankster loved to see me laugh - Loving words to the end

How can words alone do you justice? You filled my heart and soul, my days and nights. I will carry you with me always. Your story lives on through me, through my actions. I am, today, who you saw through your eyes, a strong woman, and a better woman from knowing you. Having your love, your faith and your trust, I was a blessed woman for sharing a life with you. Discovering a love that was envied, a love that none can compare. You were a man that is every woman's desire. We pledged to the end of our days, your end came much too soon. I now live on without you here. I brag of your love, our love. I reaped the benefits; I alone shared it with you…. I alone suffer without.

ARE YOU REALLY GONE

Times seems to stand still and only a moment has passed since we talked

Since I touched you, since you held me in your arms, told me you love me

Didn't I just laugh and something you said or did

I still feel your kiss on my lips

I heard you say "you look beautiful my darling"

Wasn't that this morning

I saw your eyes and the way the light up when I walked into the room

I saw your smile

I'm waiting for my morning call wasn't it yesterday you called to say hi

Are you really gone? How can that be? I swear it was just a moment ago

9/29/2011 – I've kept Rick's cell phone, I just can't bear to cancel it yet. Today there was a message from an old work buddy. I listened and the message really touched my heart and showed what an impression Rick left on people. I'll paraphrase – 'hey Rick wanted to get back to you - I kept your message for the last year and didn't want you to think I forgot about you'. I called him back to tell him that Rick had passed away. We talked for a few minutes and he told me of the fun they had in the beginning of their appraiser days. He said Rick had left a message, back in 2009, to thank him for a job referral and the message was so nice he said he had to keep it. All this time has gone by and he did not want to forget; this is how Rick affected everyone he knew. He left a lasting memory and such an impression on him. Rick's story lives on in all of his friends; he truly was bigger than life. For me my life has been changed forever; imagine how I feel every day without him. If Rick touched this person's life so much that he kept a message for over a year, how can I ever have a day without thoughts of him.

10/1/2011 – October – where has the year gone? I don't remember much of the past eight months I've been here frozen in time. Through the snow storms the rain and the unbearable heat it seems like it all happen in just weeks not months. I've watched it all pass me by, just sitting here staring out the windows. No long walks, no sunbathing or dozing on my patio and now Fall is here. Soon I will be trapped once again by winter months of cold. Rick died almost nine months ago and my life stopped on that day too. All the things I liked to do - we liked to do - I think of them I just can't bring myself to enjoy anything. The sun is shining the skies are clear and the temperature is perfect for long walk, I just don't want to leave the house. That statement is weird, if you really think about it; I leave the house every day I go to work I run errands and even visit friends so why is it so difficult to do something or go someplace Rick and I once enjoyed. I've walked along the river several times my heart is heavy and all I do is think about Rick and I being there together. I've not yet figured out what stops me from enjoying days like this. Am I just being lazy now? I think I miss sharing the experience.

After I wrote this I decided, what the hell just get outside and walk for a bit it will feel good to get moving. As I was changing my clothes I suddenly broke down and started sobbing. Not only am I afraid to do things on my own I have a fear I'll start enjoying it. Even though Rick is not with me, it will be OK to still enjoy the outdoors. I almost feel as if I'm cheating on him, that it's wrong, and the guilt and pain hit me and stop me in my tracks. I've been saying I do not want to live without Rick, that I couldn't live without him - I guess I'm afraid to prove that statement wrong.

Well I did it, I went for a long walk and it felt good. The world did not come to an end and I feel better for getting some air and sun. I even said hello to some neighbors I only knew from waving to them in the car. This is my life now, one step at a time, face the fear and find yourself. Life goes on whether you want it to or not

10/3/2011 – As I'm driving home from work I could feel the tension building inside of me the anger and frustration were right on the edge. I've imagined myself yelling out, where can I yell and scream and not have someone run to my rescue? Well, out it came as I'm driving. I just start yelling - I hate this! Hate it! Hate it! Stupid! Stupid! How could you be dead?! Now I'm crying and I look around and I see that there are cars near me and I get control for a moment. Alone again on the road I let out a scream, I'm talking loud from deep inside. Yikes, it hurt my throat and it didn't even ease my tension. I'm home now and my mood has turned dark. I start to yell again asking – why? Why? Why did you leave me? I want answers now! Where are you and why won't you talk to me?! I'm crying hard and a wailing sound is coming out of me from deep inside my anguished soul. It's loud and piercing and I rock back and forth just moaning and continuing to wail and cry. You promised me!! You promised me you would be here! We were so lost the first half of our lives; we had the second half together to get it right. We should have had another 40 years, a whole lifetime to be together. Forever you said. The moaning takes over now the pain is pouring out of me, I don't care who hears me. I'm sitting, hands over my face, rocking back and forth. Just let it all out let it drain me; this has been bottled up for too long. Finally it stops I'm worn out my throat is raw. I can't share these emotions with anyone. I've never cried like this around my family or friends only when I'm alone. It's too much to reveal, I'm not sure if anyone could handle it although a hug right now would be nice.

10/4/2011 – I told a stranger today that Rick had passed away; it's still hard for me to say. After I say it I didn't know what else to say. I like having the sympathy I will admit that. Now someone new will tell me how sorry they are, but, after that it's as if I have nothing else to say. We were having a nice chat about her being a new employee and that we should get together one night. We talked a little bit about working out and some of our interests. I tell her I haven't really worked out for many months that my life had taken a bad turn. Then I say it – 'my husband passed away'. We have few exchanges and all how difficult it is losing a spouse. And then I say - well I don't want this to get depressing I'll talk to you later and I just walk away. She'll probably not want to go for drinks now!

10/8/2011 – I sprinkled a few of Rick's ashes into our pond today. I sat out in the back for awhile and I was so calm. It was the right time to put his ashes out there. I hope I feel his energy now when I sit on the patio.

10/10/2011 – I had some time to kill before a doctor appointment, so I took a ride to the river. I decided to walk to the bridge; I like to talk to Rick from there. It's when you don't plan something that something special happens. As I was walking and talking to Rick an eagle flew alongside of me and I knew then it was him answering me. His spirit is always with me.

RIVERS EDGE

Walking along the river's edge

Leaves crunch beneath my feet - Moving at a slow steady pace

My heart is heavy yet I know where I'm heading

Sky turning shades of pink, as the sun takes her nightly dip

Standing on the bridge I ask

Are you there I've come to talk

Are you listening I have questions

I'm lost will you guide my way - I'm scared will you protect me

I'm weak share your energy with me

Shine your light on me - show me I'm not alone

You're my guardian angel now

Take me into your wings - Teach me how to fly again

Are you there - are you listening

The sun is sinking lower - I start my walk back

Show me Rick - let me know you hear me - are you walking with me

An eagle flies alongside of me

Keeps pace as I walk - Then soars high and away

My step is quick and light now - A smile lights my face

My Ricky was listening as always and brought the answers to me

As the eagle soars so shall I

I'll spread my wings and have no fear to fly

Alone I can face the world - All is out there within my reach

10/19/2011 – Nine months have passed and I miss Rick more and more every day. My mind, my heart and my soul are all on the same page now. The realization of Rick's death, my eternal pain and the loss of this wonderful husband all gang up on me now. Over the months my heart would ache, but I would push the thoughts away. Thoughts would come up and the emotions would be held in. Now it all comes together, there's no denying it no pretending it's a bad dream. He's not working at his desk or in the other room; Ricky is gone from my life forever. I will be surrounded by his love and I'll carry him in my heart and soul. I'm left to live on without him; his presence will be felt but not his hugs and kisses. His laughter will not be heard and the heat of his body never to be felt again.

The house is silent too quiet. For nine months the quiet deafened me, it's time to find my voice again, my rhythm - my beat. There is joy in life and nature I just need to open my eyes and heart and let it in. I can feel the fear in the pit of my stomach as I write these words; I'm terrified to take the steps. I feel like I'm leaving Rick, we vowed our lives to each other. I will always look to him for guidance and he'll give me the answers I need. This loneliness will propel me forward, not out of desperation but the desire to survive. This will take some time and I'm sure I'll stumble. Something is pushing me to move on, to find what I can be now. Rick always believed in my strength, it's time I do too. My future is out there I'll listen for clues and see where they take me.

10/22/2011 – The Orioned Meteor shower was last night. I woke about 5am, and with sleepy eyes kept watch for the streaking meteors. I was about to give up and said 'oh well, I guess your Bunny is not meant to see any tonight'. I waited a few more moments and sure enough a meteor streaked by; I was so overjoyed I started to cry. Even one meteor was a show for me. I imagined you streaking by with it.

10/23/2011 – Remember the co-worker I suddenly told Rick had passed? I was sure she would think of me as the Wacky Widow. We saw each other and started to talk. I apologized for being so abrupt and just springing it on her like that. I explained this is still so new and I'm not sure how or when to bring it up. She understood and we made plans to go out for that drink and dinner. Whew! I could use another friend right now.

10/24/2011 – I went to my dermatologist for annual my check up. She found a suspicious mole and had the doctor look at it, turns out it was fine. This made me think, what if it was worse, what if it was a cyst or tumor. What if?? I was scared and pissed off that Ricky would not be here to comfort me and I would go through this alone. What happens when and if it is something serious? I let out a sigh of relief yet I feel so down. This is when I need Rick the most; he would have been waiting to hear the results, making sure his Bunny is OK.

11/1/2011 – the days are flying by now. I'm in a routine of going to work, maybe working out, I take my time getting home, get ready for the next day watch TV than go to bed. The quiet in the house is still so hard to get used to. The TV is on first thing in the morning and as soon as I walk in at night. There is no conversation to stimulate my brain, no hugs and kisses to distract me from plopping down in my chair. These are my days and nights for now.

I spent a couple days with Annie, she lights up my world. The darkness of my life is so obvious when I get home after these long weekends.

I had an overwhelming sense of Déjà today. I stopped to get take out at one of our favorite places and the images of Rick and I eating here and being in this neighborhood, started flooding into my mind. As I waited for my food my eyes welled up with tears and the sense of loss was almost unbearable, I burst into tears as soon as I got into my car. I cried on and off all the way home, and I stopped to sit by the river. I sat there crying asking Rick to help me and that I needed his energy. These are the moments that shake me to my core. Something triggers a memory of Rick, the way he walked with such a purpose and a bounce to his step or the way he would look at me. When I got home I took a walk and ended by the small playground and I sat on the swing. Again images of Rick and I taking a walk and also sitting on the swings filled my mind, this is when I feel most alone. Each time a reminder of us together or an image of Rick comes into my thoughts I realize that's all I have now. These images - these memories - we'll never experience it together again. It makes me sad, very sad it's not fair.

11/2/2011 - Tonight I'm going to All Souls mass. I brought some things to have blessed, shells, rocks, pictures and a necklace Rick gave me, mementos – relics the priest called them. Our memories of the departed, what we hold dear to keep them in our hearts and minds, that sounds so sad and desperate. Is this what life comes down to at the end? A small piece of rock or a shell the last thing Rick may have touched or gave to me. His life was so much more yet I cling to these relics and display them with pride. This is so Ricky, as I pointed out a unique rock that we found. That's what's left now, these memories and stories we share we laugh and we cry over. I've been to two masses since the funeral; both were to honor the dead. I sat among family & friends, stoic, not wanting to cry. As I stare out watching the procession of candles, my mind goes back to the day of the funeral words being spoken remembering the dead and hearing the eulogy in my head. I snap back to the present and inhale sharply as I hear Rick's name being read. Hands rub my back to console me as silent tears slide down my cheeks. Hearing Rick's name being read out loud by a stranger to a room filled with strangers, fills me with both pride and horror. I was proud to hear his name put out there to have him recognized, the horror - is why his name is spoken in church. This was to honor him, yes his reward for dying, we pray for his salvation, for his entrance into the kingdom of God. For just a second, I expect him to stand and acknowledge as they called out his name. Rick loved attention, I imagine him yelling out 'Yeah, I'm here'. Knowing Rick as I do, he's first in line and with his charm – he's a shoe in. I smile at the thought. Here you go universe, here he is, put him to good use - but keep him close to me.

11/3/2011 – This has already been a tough week. I'm exhausted after the mass last night; it was like being at the funeral all over again. I feel so out of sort and more agitated than normal. I finally figured it out; at this time of year Rick and I would already be planning our upcoming vacation. I know it is two months away but we would start counting the weeks and days until January. Two different thought processes are colliding in my mind right now; I should be planning our trip and dear God it's almost a year since Rick died. What! How can that be?! Instead of anticipating an upcoming vacation I'm already thinking of January 18 and what will I do on that day. How will I be and where should I be? I started thinking I should go back to Cancun. I would stay at the same resort and make peace with it all at the same beach where he died. The resort has changed hands, became an all inclusive and much too expensive maybe it's not meant to be. I can't keep obsessing about it; just let it go for now the answers will come to me. I just can't imagine sitting home alone on the anniversary date and I don't want to be at the office either. I want to face the ocean, have a good cry and say goodbye properly to Rick. I'd like to spread his ashes into the sand and his beloved ocean. Does it really need to be that exact date, and/or spot? I know the answer will come to me.

CALLED YOUR NAME

They called out your name in church tonight. The chorus sang a sad lament.

Candles were lit for all the souls.

They called out your name in church tonight.

I looked for you to walk down the aisle. What cruel trick is this?

Everywhere I looked I saw tears. I felt the familiar fear.

Is this not a joyful gather? They called out your name in church tonight.

Lift up our hearts and souls we sang.

Welcome him with open arms they prayed

As they called out your name in church tonight

Walk into the Kingdom and shine your light

11/4/2011 – 39 years ago I married my first husband Mike and 26 years ago on November 5th I watched him die. He took his last breath as I held his hand in the hospital. I know this journey is about my loss of Rick, but all the things that happened in my past have shaped who I am now. It took almost 10 years after Mike died to write a farewell letter to him. I sat on hillside in Colorado, read the letter out loud and I set him and I free that day. The grieving and guilt finally subsided and I allowed myself to continue living and enjoying life. I decided that day it was OK to continue living. I set myself on a path of healing, allowing me to come out and be who I was supposed to be. I had 10 years of soul searching, doubt, self hatred and trying to be who everyone else wanted me to be. One year and seven months later I was ready to fly and that's when I met Rick. For the next 14 years we soared to heights I never could have imagined. How will I ever recover from this loss?

11/6/2011 – it is officially Fall, we turned the clocks back and the darkness will surround me now. With dreary days and driving home the dark my mood seems to follow. The days seem to be getting harder for me. In the first months I was in shock and the horror was too much to think about. I moved through the weeks like a robot and then I was on auto drive as I had a purpose. All the paperwork, phone calls and decisions left me a little time to think and I stayed focused. Almost 10 months later I now focus on me there's not much distraction left, it's just me and the house. I move through the days sluggish and tired and my attitude of - I just don't care - has come back. Getting through this week was tough; I was anticipating the mass for Rick and thinking of Mike's death. I was feeling very alone and asking what the hell? Why can't I have a life of love and happiness? I have small tastes of it and then it's ripped away. I was married to Mike for 13 years when he died, it wasn't a perfect marriage but we grew up together in those years. Following that, I had 12 years of struggle, a bad marriage, wild living and a lot of hating myself. Then a wonderful, loving, funny man came into my life and completed my world. Finally, everything fell into place. I was loved and respected and I loved and respected myself. 14 years was not enough time and again happiness was ripped away. The holidays are right around the corner and it's tough to think about. Am I just feeling sorry for myself? I have a right to be. I'll try to stay out of the real dark places my mind can go. I miss Rick so much and it's very lonely without him here.

TIME HEALS

They say time heals all wounds. Time tortures me, mocks me.

My wounds are cutting through to my soul.

Each day takes me further and further away from you.

My pain is like a cancer racing through my body.

No stopping it, no cure for it

The cold nights are upon us again. I long for the warmth of your body.

I call out your name crying for you. Hold me! Hold me! I need you

I see your face, no, not the face I know and love

Those eyes, dead, staring - no color in your face

Where is the twinkle of your eyes? Where is that smile?

Don't look, don't remember him that way

I want my Ricky. Why was he taken from me? Why?

I let the tears flow freely

11/8/2011

ADRIFT

I go through my days adrift and lonely - Wanting what I feel is owed me

Waited my life for someone like you - I had already paid my dues

A taste of living was enough to please - A taste of love was all but a tease

I finally knew a life of bliss - Now ripped apart from that sweet, sweet kiss

Memories are all that fill my head - Your body no longer warms our bed

My heart is only filled with sorrow - And I'll be missing you tomorrow

Someday will swim across the skies comets will be ours to ride

We'll rest among hidden stars and secretly make them ours

As I lie awake in our bed at night

I'll feel you comfort me and whisper it's all right

Someday will be together again - The two of us running through the heavens

For now I walk alone - how is it that you're really gone

I look out at the night skies -I imagine those beautiful eyes

Watching me as I go through my life

Holding dearly the gift it was to be your wife

Someday will swim across the skies comets will be ours to ride

We'll rest among hidden stars and secretly make them ours

11/10/2011 – best words of songs that describe the pain -

What am I supposed to do when the best part of me was always you? (Script)

Who would have thought forever would be severed by the sharp knife of a short life? (Band Perry)

I miss the sound of your voice – the loudest thing in my head (Matt Nathanson)

11/12/2011 – Rick is a part of my life every day, I talk to him asking for help and guidance and I still tell him about my days. I wonder if my brain fully understands that Rick is not here. I catch myself, as I just did a few moments ago; looking at the urn and the pictures I have out, and for a second I wonder what is this all here for. Could part of me still be in denial? It's hard to describe the feeling. For example; as I say out loud 'OK time to go upstairs' I walked over and picked up the urn and I just stand there staring as my mind goes blank and I feel my heart skip a beat. I literally shake my head to bring myself back. The unsettled feeling stays with me I want to remember how I'm feeling at this moment. Much of my time at home I act as if Rick is here with me. Tonight I was talking him about the beautiful sunset and what I was making for dinner. It's not a real conversation, I don't hear him answer me, and I'm just making comments out loud. He was such a good conversationalist now he's a good listener. He has given me a few answers when I needed them and I'm hoping he'll be around me for very long time. Maybe my brain wants to forget, to not feel that pain just for awhile.

HAZE

I lived my life in a haze lots of late nights and parties

I thought those were my Glory days

I was too bored never comfortable at home

Yet I always woke up sad and alone

He came into my life on a beautiful spring night

He filled my days with warmth and light

Of love and hope he always spoke

Our days forever we would spend

He promised our love never to end

Living again in a haze

Late into the night I remember our days

We had love and a happy home

Once again I wake up sad and alone

Through the years he filled my heart's desire

Hearing I love you I never tired

For this one true love I waited my life

So happy the day I became his wife

Gone now are those loving days

I'm back living again in a haze

He came into my life on a beautiful spring night

He filled my days with warmth and light

Of love and hope he always spoke

Our days forever we would spend

He promised our love never to end

In one swift moment my love was gone

I'm left again to wander alone

Ripped from me was this beautiful life

His love in my heart I will always carry

And what a privilege it was to be his wife

He came into my life on a beautiful spring night

He filled my days with warmth and light

Of love and hope he always spoke

Our days forever we would spend

He promised our love never to end

Our days forever we would spend

He promised our love never to end

11/14/2011 – People say I'm returning to normal. At work I am back to normal, my day is full I'm kept busy and focused by the files around me. My brain is challenged to concentrate and get the job done; yes I'm back to normal in the office. I have a purpose and a goal while I'm there and nothing has changed around me, same people, same files, and the same duties. My family and friends are starting to say, good to see you back to normal, there's that word again. I'm there for them as much as they are for me everyone has their own crap to deal with. We talk, I listen, give advice and laugh - yes normal I guess you would call it. At home normal for me has not yet come; my purpose has not yet been recognized. My life had been shared freely given over to Rick and everything I did was for us. It was a combined purpose of pleasing me and Rick. We discussed everything as I've noted previously he encouraged and thanked me all the time. Now I'm not really taking care of me. Once I'm home my purpose and my goal is undefined. Be patient, I say to myself, you've been taking care of you and doing it a dam good job.

11/16/2011 - Rick, we were supposed to share all experiences together the rest of my life. I'm glad I was there to share experiences with you, the rest of your life.

11/19/2011 – Each month as the 18th comes around my world is thrown off kilter. I remember every moment of January 18 and for at least 24 hours I relive the tragedy. I remember how beautiful the day was and how excited we were about the resort, breakfast and the huge beach. Time grinds to a halt and frame by frame the day goes through my mind. How happy we were together already making plans for next trip unaware of the horror in front of us. And every month I ask, how can this be? Some days I feel so strong and so confident, that I can move forward and take charge, that I am the woman Ricky saw. Some days, not so much, the fear and loneliness gather around me and I can't see beyond it. I know Rick wants me to go on, he knows he is in my heart forever. I imagine him watching over me and feeling both sadness and pride, it pains him to see me cry and he can feel my love for him. He's proud of his Bunny, taking care of herself and all her responsibilities. He does not want me to live in this sadness forever yet I know he does not want me to forget him. Have no fear Ricky, I will always love you and remember the wonderful man I was married to, my partner - my love - my best friend.

11/20/2011 - Is there a God? What is God? How can such horrible events, happen in such good people's lives. Death has been all around me this year.

How can He, in His infinite wisdom, allow this to happen? Will we, in our final moments, see the light and receive the answers that we seek? What, or who will greet us? Will our souls still be as we are now, or will we become the great hum of energy that moves through this universe? I ask these questions in earnest. My faith and my belief have been truly tested. In the past 12 months, the - Only the Good Die Young- theory has been proven. Too many taken too soon.

11/21/2011 – In my darkest loneliest moments I miss Rick's kisses, his warmth and our passion. I'll never feel him again, his arms around me and the way he held me leaving me to feel empty as I hunger for his touch. I cry….

11/23/2011 – I've had a couple "strange" occurrences. I was on the phone with Amber then static started and I heard a deep voice say hello twice. I can hear Amber saying you're breaking up I can't hear you, it cleared up and we finished our conversation. A few minutes later, as I'm watching TV, I hear a scratchy gurgling sound; I mute the TV and realize it's coming from my phone. I look and I'm not connected to a call, I can see my screen saver. I slowly put the phone to my ear and say hello, I hear nothing but that sound. I hit the end button a couple of times and finally shut the phone off. Eerie!

Tonight I was talking with Quinn about how safe Rick always made me feel. He asked if I thought Rick was with me, I answered yes I do. Do you feel safe he asks, yes I do, it's like I'm a tiny dancer held in his hands. I'm not sure why I phrased it that way; it's not exactly how I would think of Rick. As I got into the car, I put on the radio….yep…Elton John is singing Tiny Dancer. I hear you Rick, I'm listening.

11/24/2011

THE FOG

The clouds block the sun form our eyes

The fog in my head veils my vision of the future

The past is further and further behind me

As I look back I see the road I've traveled

Memories of each stop along the way

The map ahead of me not yet laid out

Yet I move forward - tentative steps gathering courage

Waiting for my vision to clear

11/25/2011 – I went downtown with my sisters, Sammie & Tom to shop and see all the Christmas decorations. We walked to the Michigan Ave. Bridge and I released some of Rick's ashes into the air and the river as we all bid him farewell.

Fly Ricky – catch the swirl of the wind and the rush of the water. Wind your way through your beloved city. Revisit our spot, touch where we once stood, and hover where we professed our love. Gather with the souls and the watchful eyes as they too protect their loves. As I walk these streets, the warm sun will be a kiss from you and a gentle breeze will be as you stroke my hair.

11/26/2011 – Cold, rainy, blustery weather, it seems like yesterday I was looking out at the gloom wondering if the mood would ever be lighter. 10 months later life is still dreary and cold. It's four weeks until Christmas; I've always loved the holidays - but not so much right now. I turn off the Christmas music; I could care less about decorating and I'm debating about putting up my tree.

11/27/2011 - I decided to put the tree up, not really for the holiday spirit, trying to make the house look cheery. I took out a few things that meant the most to me and to us, our ornaments that we collected over the years and the picture you put together for me on our first Christmas. A few times I felt your input and I put more decorations on the tree than I had planned, something kept pushing me to add more. The tree looks pretty, lights up the house but not my heart.

11/28/2011

DROWNING

Help! I feel as if I'm drowning in a sea of despair

Oh – how cliché what's that you say

You saw me smiling you heard me laughing

Can you see the twisted remnants of my heart

Can you hear the wailing of my soul

The face you see is nothing but a front - The smile holds the tears at bay

Pain courses through my veins like Cancer

Growing stronger trying to take control

My heart beats out its mourning song - Calling for its lost love

Eyes look past the beauty of life - Seeing only the Horror of Death

I shall sink into the Darkness - Block out all around me

Blissful ignorance deny me the truth

Eyes wide open I see the Horror of Death

My heart shatters my soul weeps

11/29/2011

DARK

Dark dark nights - Why do you haunt me still

Dark dark mornings - Why do you hate me still

Night void of the moon - Sun hidden from the days

Cold cold winter you mock me now

12/4/2011 – OMG! This year has sucked! Just received a call that Nicks brother John passed away, he too lost his battle with Cancer, another one taken too soon. Christmas and New Year are right around the corner, ugh, how can we celebrate? This year can't end soon enough, on to 2012 please.

12/5/2011 – I turn the lights on the Christmas tree on every morning and every night. I try to sit in the quiet dark morning and enjoy the tree as Rick and I would have; I only last a few moments and I felt like crying. It just reminded me I'll never sit with Rick again and that made me sad. I carry that sadness all day today and did not feel like talking much. I have a terrible kink in my neck the stress feels heavy and my mood shows it. I don't want to feel the pain anymore please let me go numb for awhile.

12/6/2011 – Rick I professed to my love for you every day, I will profess my love for you through eternity.

The burden of life weighs heavy on me. You always carried the weight, you were my support. Did I ever thank you? I now know the strength you had every day, I love you for taking life on for us and the energy you gave. I miss you now more than I can say, show me the way Rick, help me find my strength to face life without you.

12/7/2011 – another husband is gone too soon another wife mourning her loss the world around me is flooding in tears

John's wake is tonight I cry for him and for his family's' sorrow, they too know the pain of loss.

12/12/2011 I spent another day with Annie, as I'm driving, I feel the heaviness creep back in as I get closer to home. The silence hits me as I walk in the door. Realizing, again, how alone I feel. My spirits are low and time drags on. When will I be comfortable with me?

12/15/2011

WHERE YOU ARE

A perfect couple some would say

Not everyone got us we knew right away

Our love grew fast and strong

Days and nights blend into one - A pledge to eternity became our song

I'll beg and plead - bargain with my soul

If I could change the events of that fateful day

Having you next to me holding you in my arms

Worth any price asked of me to pay

Take me where you are I know it's not my time

I'm waiting here for you until our souls meet again

You satisfied my hunger overflowing from your love

Thirst quenched by your kiss

Now left craving and parched my heart shall diminish

You brought the sun into my life - The stars all seemed so bright

Now I walk these days with clouds in my eyes

Not seeing the sun or stars for my nights

Take me where you are I know it's not my time

I'm waiting here for you until our souls meet again

I pray to God to help me on my knees until they bleed

Even He can't answer this desire no matter how I cry and plead

You have left me much too quickly how do I now go on alone

Yours was the love I longed for - Our life complete in our happy home

Take me where you are I know it's not my time

I'm waiting here for you until our souls meet again

Take me where you are I die every day without you

Take me where you are I'll be waiting here for you

Our souls will meet again

12/16/2011 – Today was the annual Christmas cookie baking day with my sisters. What a great day of laughing and a lot of baking. I have no idea what I'm doing with all these cookies, they are hard to resist. I used to hide them from Rick, now; I'll have to hide them from me.

12/17/2011 –I went to the Bersani Christmas party at Gloria's. I told them, being with the Bersani's is like a big warm embrace. I'm so at ease around them and they love to talk about Rick, stories were shared some funny some just memories about him. I envied all the couples as I watched them interact. All the young ones with their whole life in front of them, there was so much love in the room. It was hard to say goodbye and head home to an empty house.

12/18/2011 – It's been 11 months, shocking to think the year is coming to an end. Again, I was thinking about how we would be planning what to do on vacation by now, we've been doing that for eight years and now I feel lost and the void is so obvious. I was cleaning and running up and down stairs, suddenly I just stopped as if I was forgetting to do something. I realized how imbedded in my brain vacation planning has been. The two of us would sit in front of the Christmas tree, and make our 'what do we need for the beach' list. The next few weeks will be hard; I'm trying to be in the holiday spirit

The lights on the tree are spotlights into the darkness of my soul.

12/19/2011 – Christmas 2011

Them - Twinkling lights, fresh baked cookies, carolers, harried shoppers, dinner feasts, gathering of friends, blanket of snow, children laughing.

Me – cold days, early darkness, needless spending, mindless eating, bundled up, cabin fever, crowded malls, no joy in shopping.

12/20/2011 – What the hell is going on?! I got a call that a friend of mine Dick, just died of cancer. What's with taking all the men in the prime of their live??!!

12/21/2011 – I'm desperately avoiding being alone with my thoughts; it's too much to bear thinking of the holidays and not having Rick here and the one year anniversary of his death. My mind is in overdrive I'm more forgetful and flustered. I'm trying to stay so busy or occupied; when thoughts do manage to creep in I'm lost in tears. My eyes can't take anymore crying, I'm tired, exhausted and short tempered. I got lots of Christmas cards they're nice but I don't want to read them. I look to see who they're from and toss them aside, lots of smiling faces and happy families, too difficult to look at. It's hard to think about anything these days; the smallest thing will bring a familiar sting of tears.

12/23/2011 – Survival - I know how to survive. I survived Mike being sick for years, watching him die and becoming a young widow. I survived a bad abusive marriage and divorce. I survived alone until I met the man I was meant to be with. I finally had what I yearned for, a wonderful man, a happy marriage a partner for life and most of all I found myself. I was happy, content and a true partner to Rick. Yes I survived all of my past horrors and mistakes and I made it on my own. I got a good job, bought my own house, had a group of friends and I was managing and surviving. But, how do I survive the loss of Rick?! I can manage alone; I just don't want to, I want Ricky in my life. I've made it through this year, yet I'm barely surviving. I'm buried in darkness, clawing my way out. I beg for light and to breathe fresh air, to wake from this nightmare and learn to really smile again, to see the beauty in nature and feel my heart beat again. I don't want to just survive I want to live

If using the word easier applies then yes it was easier to get through the past. I was younger, full of life and I knew or hoped I had many years ahead of me. I was hopeful and eager to start a new life after my divorce. I was 45 when I met Rick and full of life and energy. Now I'm 60, my future seems so uncertain and death has been all around me. Looking ahead, I only see the loneliness. I used to have a 'live for today' attitude, I went at life with full abandonment, and it was mine for the taking. Rick and I enjoyed every moment together. I was quick to laugh and embrace life, loved nature and lived to the fullest. That was my life, our life and we deserved it. It was supposed to be that way to the grave. Ricky died too soon and now life has gone dark.

12/25/2011 – Christmas morning I woke up in Sammie's bed, not where I expected to be. Rick and I should be sipping coffee and reading our cards to each other. I got here last night and Patty and I went to mass. It was lovely, I forgot how beautiful Christmas mass is, all the decorations and singing the hymns are good for the soul. I prayed asking Mary to watch over him and I asked him to keep me safe and let his presence be known. Sammie gave up her bed for me, she said I should stay the night; her plan is to get me drunk and enjoy myself. As much as I love my family and have fun with them I'm missing Ricky so much today, all of our little traditions and how we felt so blessed to have each other. Today I feel like we're going through the motions, we've all had our losses this year both Bill and Nick lost a brother. I believe a spouse is much harder and the suffering takes longer to get through. I feel like half of me is missing tonight. I put a smile on, laugh at the silliness and do my best to enjoy the day. It was so hard to leave the house yesterday everything felt wrong. I'm going alone and I'm not coming home, I feel like I'm deserting Rick and I cried as I walked out the door. I know he's with us watching me with my sisters, as he always got a kick out of us together. I should be home waking up with him, it all just feels so wrong. Merry Christmas my Darling - I love you

12/26/2011 – After all the hype and worry, Christmas came and passed, it was just another day to get through without Rick being part of it. During the meal no prayers were said, no thanks were given and no mention of any of the departed. I made a silent toast to the boys that were lost that year.

During the evening we have fun playing games I drank too much and stayed up way too late. Christmas or not, Rick was not there with us and the void was obvious.

12/28/2011 - The Christmas tree symbolizes the brightness and lighthearted spirit of our home. It shows individuality and unique can come together in a cohesive beautiful picture. That's what our tree has, that's why it been so difficult for me to sit with them. It seems one sided - off kilter just as I am now. Rick and I, as in all things of our life, came together and created our own unique beauty. As I appreciate all of what we had, the tree is the symbol that reminds me of what is now lost. A glaring reminder, and yes, it makes me sad and angry. How can there be such a light in a world that is so dark to me. I've been unable to direct my anger toward anyone or anything. The tree gave me my outlet. That tree became my metaphor for life and now death. I always felt the Christmas tree "lit up" our life now it glares at the darkness.

12/31/2011 – New Years Eve – I had great plans for this day, the end of the year. I decided to stay home all weekend and face the New Year with a new purpose, so strong and sure of myself. I planned on walking along the river; it was to be sunny and warm today, well the sun is nowhere to be found and it is cold and foggy. I was to make myself a good healthy meal to end the old and start the new. Soon after I got up, it was obvious I'm sick, chills - headache - scratchy throat and very tired. 1:00 PM I haven't moved from my chair I'm wrapped in a blanket and I needed a nap. Not how I planned to celebrate the New Year. I will push on and at least get some food in the house.

Its 4:00 PM I made it to the grocery store and drove to the river. I stood on the embankment and I wished for a happy new year. I said to Rick 'this is the end of the year, the final goodbye to 2011. I'm ready to start fresh and face the coming year with a purpose. Ricky - be my strength when I'm worn down, the air that I breathe and the light that shines in my heart". It seems a perfect day to say goodbye to this past year. As I look at the bare trees, darkened waters' and gloomy skies, I can only wish for brighter days. The rebirth of life is what we crave on these dark winter days. Spring will be right around the corner and my days will be filled with color.

This past year I've barely been living, I do not remember much of my days, nothing really stands out. My birthday was probably the only experience I enjoyed and the birth of Annabelle. That's the point, I'm living but I'm not experiencing life. Every day with Rick was living life to the fullest and experiencing every moment. I looked forward to my morning hugs and kisses, Ricky teasing me and my midmorning phone call from him, just to say hi and that he loved me. I would wonder what else the day would bring, talking about current events and him wanting to hear about my day. I can go back and recount our talks our lovemaking and all of our fun. I finally got to have a rich, full life. Now, I hardly remember what day it is or what I did last week, this has been my life - if you can call it that. I've been sitting here reflecting on my time with Rick and how we would make it our experience, unique to us, non conformant. I'm numb, sleepwalking my days and dreamless sleep at night. One year ago we were dancing in our living room; we were singing, eating and drinking wine. We drank too much and barely made it to midnight but we lived, we experienced and we looked forward to the next time. Not a care in the world starting 2011, we were leaving in 14 days for Cancun. I want that night back! I want this year back! Make it 12/31/2010 please! I've been asleep for a year and never waking up again. Now, the tears start!

12:05 AM - 2012 has arrived, ushered in by the distant booms of fireworks and neighbors shouting out. As I end a long year of sadness and heartbreak, I start a new year the same. My heart aches and I long for Rick's arms to hold me tight, to hear him whisper I love you Darling - Happy New Year.

1/2/2012 – So far I'm facing the New Year with clean up and clean out. The biggest accomplishment is that I finally unpacked Rick's suitcase. Yes, it's been in the house, still packed since January of 2011. I unpacked it and just bagged up his clothes, I can't bear to look at or get rid of them. I sorted some of his stuff to give to charity; a lot of his clothes still hang in the closet, too much to go through right now. I want to do more, but the body seems to be slowing down. I think I need to sit back and take in what I've done so far, I feel good, no tears but a little shaky.

1/3/2012 – I'm in a state of confusion my senses are at odds with the battle of mind and heart. All my brave talk of starting fresh, moving forward into the New Year, leaves my mind over thinking and my heart weeping. I feel like I'm leaving Rick behind.

1/10/2012 – I can't believe a week has passed. I think I'm shutting down my feelings, just like before the holidays. My anticipation of what the one year anniversary will be like is getting to me. I've had such heartburn or something similar for a few days now and my nerves are getting the better of me.

I had a few awkward moments with a friend of mine at work; she's been very short with me. When I came into the office on Friday I had a voice mail telling me that I have not been a very good friend and that I'm not the asking about her. Really! I had talked with her couple weeks ago; I admitted that I was withdrawn, that the holidays and all the happiness are just too much for me. I apologized up front for being quiet or bitchy that my mood swings were unpredictable. After hearing the message I wrote her a card saying I was sorry and I re-explained my feelings. That I feel jealous about all the talk of Christmas and what everyone's been doing over the holidays. I told her she was important to me and thanked her for being a support person. After a long weekend off, I came in and she is not talking to me. It would be such a shame to have a 20 year relationship come to an end over this.

1/14/2012 – I woke early this morning and thought back to a year ago, when Rick and I were eager to get started on our vacation. It was snowing a lot and we wondered if our flight would be on time, or worse, canceled. If I could go back to that morning knowing what I now know I would've prayed for a blizzard. I'm so focused on January 18th, I realized today the next 10 days I will be reliving the horror. I'm sitting here thinking about the day we left by this time last year we had boarded our flight. We beat the crowds at security, but, Ricky got searched because of the vest he was wearing with all the pockets plus he forgot to take out his liquids from his luggage. We sat at Starbucks drinking coffee and eating the Christmas cookies and I had brought. This is going to be torture, enough to drive one insane; I just don't know how to turn it off. I want to remember, to mourn moment by moment, stop, play, and rewind that's what my mind is doing to me. For the next 10 days I will relive all those moments, my last days enjoying life with Rick and the beauty of where we were. I'll remember the grotesque sight of Rick, lying dead, alone and covered with towels. I'll remember all the days following making plans to get him home and then the funeral. I've made it through this year and I will get through these days. Rick was so proud of me and I will continue to make him proud, I'll live with grace, believe in me, know my strength, have a positive attitude and choose what's right for me in my life.

1/17/2012 – One year ago was the last time I heard Rick say Goodnight My Darling - sleep tight - I'll see you in the morning. I go to bed tonight and I put this year behind me, I'll say my goodbyes tomorrow. I need to let go of this pain, I've used it like a blanket wrapped around me for comfort, protection and to hide under. Letting go of the pain is not letting go of Rick, I hold him close in my heart and mind. I'll remember the Good Nights and I Love You; he still makes me smile as I think of him. Goodnight My Darling I'll see you in the morning.

1/18/2012 – Every day we get up and we expect life to be as usual, we take our days for granted, happily going along especially if life is good. You're in a great marriage what could go wrong? That is exactly how I felt one year ago.

It starts on January 13, when I got home from work I found that Rick had cleaned the whole house and he was in the process of packing for our trip. We're heading to Cancun and my whole house has been cleaned - life is good. Very early the next morning we're ready to leave and as we're standing by the front door, we stop and take a moment to say I love you and then we get into the cab. Several hours later we're in Cancun walking barefoot down the beach. The next four days we relaxed, ate well, took long walks and just enjoyed being together. January 18, Tuesday morning, we head to the Hilton, there are blue skies temperature is rising it's a beautiful sunny day. We sat down for huge buffet and enjoyed every bite of it. We were anxious to hit the beach as we walked the grounds admiring the splendor. We picked our spot well away from the crowds and we went shell and rock hunting. Rick wanted to get into the water, that was the whole reason we came to the Hilton not only did they have a spectacular beach the waves were perfect for body surfing. Rick was trying to convince me to come in the water with him, I actually considered it. He was pretending I was a hot babe that had been sent to him by the concierge, he flirted, kissed me and then pinched my butt - little did I know how much that memory would mean to me. Once we get down to the water I chickened out, the water was deeper and the waves were a little too high for me to be comfortable in. I tried to get him to go further down the beach; it seemed a little calmer down there. Nope! It was too crowded for him, he liked his space. One more kiss and I watched him jumping over the waves as he headed out, dunking under the water and letting the waves carry him several times. He waved as usual, kept jumping and going under the water as I stood watching from the shore. Suddenly my heart skipped a beat, something looked wrong – off - he was just standing there and not moving at all. I gestured with my hands to say 'what?' he just stood there looking down. I thought he saw something and again I shrugged and put my hands up to ask 'what?' He motioned oddly with one hand as I'm standing on the shore asking out loud – What? What? Do you see something? He fell forward, I thought he was looking at something under the water but in a few moments panic set in and I knew something was terribly wrong. I took a step into the water and quickly realized I could not help or get to him. I start to panic and I cry out for help, one minute he's waving to me, the next, he collapsed in the water. He's now floating in front of me, suddenly a young man rushes in, grabs Rick's arms and pulls him up, and his color was so pale. NO! I see his eyes…they're gone - the beautiful light is gone. I'm screaming over and over "don't you leave me Rick". The only thing I could do was retrieve his goggles from the water. Our beautiful sunny day has gone black. It went from watching my love at one with the ocean, to him now dying in front of me. What started as a morning of bliss and laughter has turned into a screaming horrible nightmare. The man I love, the man I waited all my life for, my love, my protector, and my partner forever, died on a beautiful day at that spectacular beach. I stood there crying helplessly watching as others try to save him. I knelt at his side holding his hand, begging him not to leave me, telling him I love him. I was pulled away as they pumped his chest and tried to breathe life into him; I screamed his name over and over. I feel like I'm watching it from afar, Rick is

92

lying on the beach covered by towels and all I could do was scream and cry. Why was I not by his side? I could not bear to look at him; he was bruised and scraped up from being dragged up the beach and from the medical team working on him. I'm sorry for not holding you then. I can see the bruising on his chest from the compressions and on his face from the oxygen they were trying to get to him. I watched as they all walked away leaving him lying there alone as the tide started to come in. I'm hysterical and trying to remember phone numbers to call, somehow I remember Cindy's work number and they call her. I don't even remember talking to her, and then Patty is on the phone trying to calm me down, I only remember her saying "breathe Janice breathe". People are all around me, holding me, comforting me, praying with me. Not me….HELP RICK! God surrounded me with Angels to keep me calm and take care of me. I was being taken care of by many people and you were all alone. I asked them to move you because the water was coming up, instead they piled a bunch of towels around you and said they could move you until the coroner arrived. You were left like a pile of seaweed on the shore, I'm sorry they couldn't help you, I'm sorry you were left alone. You carried yourself in life with such dignity I'm so sorry for the undignified way you died. He's being taken away now and I'm not allowed to go with, where… when will I see him?! I'm ushered into a car with four strangers; I will spend the next twelve hours with this group. Finally, I talk to Armond, Rick's brother, he's getting on flight as soon as possible, and I'm left to make decisions on my own. Police station…making a statement…to the funeral home…making arrangements to get him home. The morgue….the horror! Won't go in…can't go in! The funeral director claims his body. I'm numb now...how can this be…wake up – this must be a nightmare. 10pm at funeral home, Rick's brother Armond and Kitty arrive, a friend of mine Gene, who lives in Cancun, also arrives. Rick's body is ready for us…Gene and Armond hold me up. The four people from the hotel who have been my support all day and have kept me sane, read bible verses as the priest blessed Rick, PLEASE WAKE ME UP! I can't even cry my mind will not believe what it's seeing. I stand there staring at what looks like Rick, but it just can't be.

We're leaving now, leaving Rick in this place. I won't see him again until we're home at the funeral. Late at night, I wake up looking for Rick, he must be here. I yell out at the sky & ocean, filled with anger that you've been taken. I think of you alone and praying you weren't scared. The fear sets in and I begin to cry. I scream out and cry through the night....alone now...alone.

One year ago January 18, 2011 Ricky lost his struggle to hold on to life.

Rick died doing what he loved most, playing in the water; the reality of that is still hard for me to accept. It all happened right front of me yet I don't want to believe it. The autopsy said he choked to death, I guess we'll never know what really happened. I had to trust the autopsy; I could not bear to bring it to court to ask for another. It could have been days waiting in Mexico for the court to decide, the result would be the same....Rick died. I lost my love, my life, my Ricky. I lost the love of my life and world lost a beautiful soul. I'm sure he's watching over me and if he can he'll be by my side always, he was such a strong life force and I believe he lives all around me.

One year I've gone without your kisses, hugs, hearing your voice your laugh or feeling your body next to mine. I've endured sleepless nights, a cold bed, an empty house, lonely hours, an aching heart and countless tears. Living without you is the hardest thing I've had to do. Yes, I lived without you most of my life but now knowing what I've lost makes life unbearable. I'm honored I was your wife your love. I'm so fortunate to have had those years with you it should have been more. You are my heart, mind, and soul. You were my calm, my rock, my strength. I will miss that smile and the way you could make me laugh. My love is yours....forever and ever. Today is about us, our love, our life, my loss, my sorrow, looking forward and gaining strength to see tomorrow.

I did a lot of different things today. I made a video montage, pictures of our life together, which I narrated and set to the music of Tinas "The Best" it goes like this:

THE STORY OF RICK AND JAN

We met May 11, 1997 our first date was May 17th. We knew, after that night, we would be together forever. We got engaged August 20, 1999 and we were married May 12, 2001. When we first met "Simply the Best" was our description of each other and our relationship. We decided that would be our entrance song for our wedding. As we danced into the reception hall, everyone was on their feet cheering and yelling. We set the tone for the evening and the rest of our lives. We lived happily ever after, bought our home and went on some great trips. We loved each other madly. Our story comes to a tragic end January 18, 2011. On a beautiful beach in Cancun, my Ricky died right before my eyes. As he did in life, I know he'll always be watching over me and be by my side. After all, he was Simply the Best.

I went to mass at St. Marcelline, the church we got married at. I went to breakfast alone, a new experience for me and I wasn't sure what to do with myself, it's nicer to have a companion. Ironically, the couple sitting behind me is having an argument as I reflect on how wonderful Rick and I were together.

I went to Chandler's where we held our reception, walked around the snow covered grounds and scattered some of Rick's ashes where the flower beds would be. Later I took a walk along the river in West Dundee it's a very cold and snowy day. I ended the day with a spa pedicure.

The memories throughout the day made me cry and smile. I smile remembering our wedding, the fun we had and the wonderful life we shared and I cried for my loss of it all.

If you take anything away from this past year it should be never take a day for granted. Celebrate life, laugh hard, love deeply, say I love you and hug every day. Rick and I live our lives together in love. Yes as any couple there were moments we may have been bitchy, disagreed or ignored but we recognized and acknowledged our feelings, said I'm sorry and meant it. We never forgot to say thank you darling or I love you. Those were the last words we spoke to each other. When he complemented me on the beach, moments before he went into the water, saying to me what a hot chick I was, I laughed, I kissed him and thanked him. As he went into the water we both said I love you had our last kiss and I felt the last pinch of my butt. These were all the things we took for granted, I assumed he would be grabbing at me at least another 30 years. I miss everything I had with Rick, his quirks, his habits, his goofy sense of humor, our talks, his loyalty, the way he truly loved me and mostly I miss his hugs and kisses. We never went very long into our day without a kiss, a hug or just a gentle touch. I still imagine him, as he would say goodbye each morning, standing in the foyer every day saying to me 'you look beautiful I love you darling'. We would stand together, hug for a long moment and kiss three times. Some mornings I stand in our spot close my eyes and pretend he's right there. I kiss the air three times hoping he can sense it and I never walk out without saying goodbye - I love you. Every day for the past year it's been the same as I walk out or come home, always saying goodbye or hi honey hoping to hear his voice one more time saying back to me hi honey or I love you. I'm greeted by silence, no open arms, no smile or no kiss. At least I have videos from our trips to always hear and see him. It's still hard to admit I'll never feel his touch again.

1/19/2012 – Today is the first day of the second year without Rick. Last year I sat in the lobby of the Hilton and made plans for getting Rick home and planning the funeral. I was numb moving through the motions, my mind protecting me from going insane. Everyone was moving around me happy, smiling and enjoying the Mexican sun, unaware of the nightmare running in my head. I'm sitting here today looking out at a dreary snow filled day remembering the warmth of the sun and how blue the sky was. I hated it, did not want the sun to touch me. Mother Nature had defied me and had taken my Ricky. I hated her, all of nature and any force out there was now my enemy. I denied all beliefs that day and many days to follow. The ultimate power of the Universe had ripped Rick from our lives and held him in a cold - cold grip. I denounced the belief that "he's in a better place" Ha! What better place for Rick than by my side? This is where he belongs, he was happy, living his world as he pleased. My faith had been tested, I could not pray. I placed my anger against the Universe. How could I pray, or ask for guidance, I felt betrayed and could not trust the answers that would be sent to me. I talked to Rick every day and still do. I will always trust and believe him. Everything I had believed about faith, Guardian Angels, God and the power of the Universe turned their backs on us when we needed them most. Everyone said the Angels were there with me that day. Where were they for Rick? I would have been fine, I begged for help asking him not to die, praying for him to live, I was denied and he was taken. Just like that, in a split moment of time, he's gone never to be heard, seen or felt again. So, I went to church asked Mary to bring peace and calm to my heart and mind, guide me and show me how to live with grace. I prayed to keep Rick in the arms of Jesus. Send me messages let me know his spirit is still alive.

The anger is still there. Ricky lost the chance to live out the dreams he had for us, yet I'm the one filled with anger and despair. I honored and will continue to honor his life. I'm left with a broken heart and unfulfilled promises. So, yeah I'm pissed and I'm making it about me.

One year later and I have no idea what to do with my days and nights. How long do I sit in silence?! I'm frozen in time unable to imagine what my life can or will look like. I need a reason for the way things have to be and I wait for a sign to show me my new path; I have to be ready to see it and walk down it.

1/24/2012 – The one year anniversary of your wake, it was the first time in a week that I got to see you and touch you. That's all I can think about this morning, one year ago I saw you lying in a coffin. I don't remember much of the wake I just know I never left your side that night, not even to use the restroom. Food and water was brought to me but I would not leave that room. I placed some of your favorite things in the coffin - sunglasses, shells, pictures and of course rocks. You looked so handsome I was rubbing your head and your chest kissing you goodbye then I went home to bed.

The funeral was the 25th I asked for the songs Into the Mystic and The Best played. I remember thinking what's wrong with me no tears, no sobbing, I'm staying strong I want to remember every moment, and I do. A year has passed yet I can remember the cold air as I got out of the car, saying my final goodbye to you, talking to you and telling you how much I love you, that your Bunny will be OK she'll miss you, kissing you over and over and stroking your face, Cindy pulling me away telling me it's time to go, I remember it all. One year later I'm living it all over again. I took today off to honor you to remember you and finally let the tears and sobbing come.

1/29/2012 – I sit paralyzed, my mind telling me to move, do something – anything, and just move. My body will not cooperate; I lay on the bed staring at the ceiling. I remember finally coming home a year ago for the first time, I had spent a couple extra days at Patty's, plus I was sick. Home alone, the only sounds are the echoes of my screams in my head. No matter how tight I squeeze my eyes shut the images of Rick dying; lying in a casket will not go away. One year later those sights and sounds still haunt me. The realization of isolation and loneliness hits me hard. Just when I think I'm taking a step forward I stumble, fall and crawl back to the dark safe place I've sat in all year. I started my day with the right intentions, let's clean out some drawers. OK, one drawer open and can't decide what to keep or throw out. I found an old book, throw that out – done. I'm bored what now? Let's look in the cabinets downstairs, found some old cookbooks, looked at a couple I'm not going to use and put on the stack for charity - done. Well here I am lying in bed doing nothing except writing my thoughts. I want to be outside feel the warmth of the sun. Today is deceiving, blue skies but cold windy temps. Winter days, and being bored, a bad combination that leads to eating and sitting around.

Why did I think it would start to be easier? I made it through the first year, the first of everything without Ricky, Birthdays, anniversary, holidays and all the other dates that meant anything to us and even the Hallmarks holidays. I went through the year in a fog; most of it has gone by so fast. I was numb and scared now I really feel a loss. I seem to be aware in a way that's more mindful that heartfelt. What I mean is - I'm focusing more on me and how to plan my future, money, health, vacations etc. I need to take on Rick's role, he would plot and plan, we would discuss, decide and he would take the actions needed, all those steps are up to me now.

Oh how I ache for Ricky daily, my heart still breaks at no goodnight kisses. My heart has been mourning the loss this past year, my brain is finally catching up. It's a new year with decisions to be made some right away others soon enough. All my papers still need to be in order and everything is still scattered around the house. Taxes are right around the corner, I need to make a will and what to do with the rental properties. I need to get myself on a budget. No more emotional spending! Enough with shoes already!

2/3/2012 – What a difference a year makes, one year ago we were under almost 2 feet of snow, brutal cold winds and huge drifts, and I was making my way back to work. I dragged myself out the door dreading the thought of seeing people, holding back tears and barely able to pull myself together. I managed; I made it through one day at a time. One year later even the weather has a brighter outlook forties today and sunny. My mood, other than UGH I have to go to work, is also lighter. We had a company party yesterday I talked, I laughed, I was relaxed and I enjoyed it. I also have a busy weekend ahead going way out of my comfort zone to watch bull riding and listen to a country band. Tomorrow I'm going out with all the girls to see Elvis Lives. Yes quite a difference, I'm slowly finding me with lots of work ahead.

2/5/2012 – Super Bowl Sunday, I'm not going anywhere but I'm OK with being home. I'm cooking and taking care of chores, I'm really OK being here alone at least today I am.

Learning to be comfortable in your own skin is hard enough as you grow up, at age 60 it's a real challenge. You think I'd know who I was by now. I struggled for years always trying to please men, be who I thought they wanted me to be, just so they would like me. With Rick it all came natural; I never pretended I was just me. It was easy Rick accepted me, all of me, anyway that I was. I saw myself through his eyes; he was my mirror now I need to find me on my own. I know it's there it always was I just don't see it yet.

2/9/2012 – As the year passed life has gone on, no matter what, life will go on with or without me. I sat frozen for a long time; unable to move forward or to change anything in my life. Somewhere in my brain I thought I could not move or change anything, that Rick would come back and not be able to find me. I could not leave him behind. It's not really getting any easier for me without having Rick in my life, time goes on and I miss him every day. I can continue to sit back and watch or I can jump back on that ride called life. My future is out there it's up to me to find it. I had great life with Rick, experiences no one else can share. All because I took the right path at the right time and put myself out there. I trusted Rick and I let him in. I'm healing, getting strong again both mentally and physically. I carry Rick's words and his beliefs in me in my heart; it's my badge of honor. It's time to start walking and opening doors - baby steps.

2/26/2012 – It has been a couple weeks since I've written, I've been keeping busy and have not taken the time to write. The up side to that, my mind has not been plagued with tormenting thoughts. I've laughed more and I feel better and more open, yet I still think about and miss Ricky every day. Through all this pain and sorrow I still find beauty in the glory of sunsets, moon lit nights, bright stars and hawks soaring overhead.

I have a secret to confess, I talked with a psychic, don't laugh or scoff, I believe. I was ready to hear and listen to my energy reading, all she knew was my first name nothing else. She talked about my pain and how it has consumed me how closed off to life I am. She saw Rick and saw him struggle; it was everything I was hoping to hear and more. Days after I realized I felt calmer my heart was not racing and my mood had lifted. I felt as if I was looking at life with eyes wide open. For the first time I knew it was OK to move forward, to look outside of my walls. I still have no idea what my path is, but I'm ready and willing to start looking forward. Ricky is in my heart and he goes with me every step I take.

I've decided not to say no, to try new things, open doors to see what is on the other side. It sounds so simple and easy, like I said before - baby steps. Some things are very simple probably no big deal, but for me it is a big deal just to get moving and put myself out there and get back to "normal". I've gone back to the gym working with a trainer and started yoga. Now I need to work on my eating habits, I know all I need to know about healthy eating, I'm just lazy about preparing, time to hold myself accountable.

I've also started a new friendship with the new attorney I met a couple months ago. Funny, it's like going on a first date; you know very little about each other and hope the conversation flows. You never know if what you like to talk about is interesting to anyone else. The fear of rejection has held me back; it's a risk I'm willing to take to get out there and meet new people. I'll be me, they can take it or leave it, they leave ...it will be their loss.

The more I get out, the more exposure to new things for me. Each door I open will lead me to a new experience or I'll reconnect with something familiar. For the first time I can honestly say I look forward to opening the next door; who knows it could be the surprise of my life. After all, that is how I met Rick, took a risk and opened the door. Look how wonderful that surprise turned out to be.

2/27/2012 – I got so caught up in the moment, so excited I'm planning for the future. I was looking forward to something new, trying new things. Suddenly my heart skips a beat, and I feel the sadness set in. This is not the future I thought I would have, my plans were already made. Take a deep breath, it will be ok….someday. Ricky is and always will be part of my life; he is in my heart and by my side. He took me on the ride of my life, and allowed me to see what life is all about. I will not allow that to die also.

2/29/2012

WINGS BROKEN

I lay a crippled and frozen - Mindless thoughts a darkened soul

In a ray of sun he came into my life

Eyes filled with promise arms to hold me tight

Slowly I mended - my heart felt free - Still afraid to fly, he gently guided me

On the edge we stood took the leap together

We flew then as one with the promise of Forever

Forever ended all too soon we came crashing down

The sun is no longer from my world he is gone

My wings now clipped my heart is broken

I rely on the memories his beautiful words spoken

I'll remember those eyes his arms so strong

His belief in me is what guides me on

I walk alone in a world left so still - I'll carry his love and re-light my soul

On his words I will feed I will always be full

3/3/2012 - I am a survivor. I have a strong will to survive. I have survived many horrible events. I am surviving. Any and all ways you can say it, I've done it, I am doing it. My strength has proven me wrong over and over. When I think I'll never go on, this is my breaking point; I push on, stand tall and walk through it. I've seen deaths, heartbreak, and had a broken soul. I suffered the loss of my one true love. I see my mind and soul – closed, dark and cold forever. My heart aches for Ricky every day. I may never recover from his death – MY LOSS. But, I will not quit life. I've come out of a dark tunnel and discovered, in all my sadness, and darkest thoughts, I want to find the joy in life again. The simple act of laughing brings life into your heart. I've realized I can laugh, truly laugh again. I enjoy the company of friends and can be in the moment.

The words and melody of the following poem just came into my head as I was driving. I recorded it and made a little photo video so I would not forget.

OPEN YOUR EYES

There's more to life than what we see - There's more to life than what we are

There's more to life than what will be

The life you live is who you are   the love you give will fill your heart

live now   love free   no fear   just be

you'll reap the joy of the love received

live now   love free   no fear   just be

Open your eyes see the world - Open your eyes receive the world - Open your eyes be the world

live now   love free   no fear   just be

you'll reap the joy of the love received

live now   love free   no fear   just be   no fear   just be

103

3/9/2012 – Went out for dinner and music with some of the girls, great oldies music that we had a blast dancing to. I looked around and noticed a few women as old as or older than me, they were quite flashy and made up with low cut tight dresses. I thought for a moment, OMG is this my future? Will I be hanging out in bars or restaurants with old single women and leering men watching us as we dance?! Everyone seemed so fake and desperate.

3/13/2012 – I pulled a muscle or something in my back and I start to cry, not from the pain but I'm pissed. Just as I was getting back into the gym, wham I'm on the sidelines. I'm crying again because I feel so vulnerable. Where's my Rick when I need him? There's no one here to comfort me, I feel small and fragile.

3/14/2012 – I just booked a trip to Cabo I feel excited, nervous and a little guilty. Before I booked it, I sat here and talked to Rick explaining how much I need this getaway. I told him I'll be safe, I'm going with Cindy and Nick. I cried as I talked to him, this was our spot our honeymoon and we went again in 2009 one of the best trips ever. I feel guilty spending the money; this is a huge step for me but worth it. I just can't keep wondering how is it going to be, how am I going to be. I will try to stay in the moment; it will be emotional with so many memories. I'll remember and a make some new ones of my own.

3/21/2012 – I feel as if I'm in a parallel universe, I go about my day and suddenly things seem very familiar and I have déjà vu. I'll have a flash of a memory but I can't quite grasp it or put my finger on it. Today as I walked to my car, my mind's eye saw the identical day but in a different place and time. As I walked I felt as if I was suddenly moved into another space and time, I have felt like this all day. At times it seemed as if I have forgotten something or I'm trying to remember a conversation I was just having, everything I did today seemed like a repeat. Looking at photos of Rick that feeling of despair comes up and my stomach lurches at the thought of never seeing that smiling face again. The sense of loss weighs heavy on me again today it seems impossible that you're gone. Some days I feel as if I've been without you for so long, day after day life has gone on. Sometimes it shocks me that it's more than a year and sometimes it feels like it's just an hour since our last kiss. I still find myself thinking of you here at home waiting for me to tell you about my day. I walked in tonight and as usual I said hello darling I'm home, one second later I asked - why didn't you say hello. The house seemed unusually quiet tonight. I miss you, I need you, and I have so much to talk to you about, visit me in my dreams tonight. I love you darling - Goodnight. I feel like crying, I want to cry, I welled up but the tears won't come. What's holding them back?

3/25/2012 – We celebrated Cindy's birthday Friday night. Went to dinner with the girls and another band was playing, we have fun and danced again. Several guys stopped by to talk to us and even danced with us. It was harmless and fun but it still felt strange. I danced with a man, talked and laughed with another and it felt odd. I tried to stay in the moment but I kept thinking Rick would not be happy, this was a little too much conversation that seemed like flirting. The place is a bit of a meat market and you do not make eye contact as you walk to the ladies room, they'll sense the weakness and pounce. It did feel good to laugh and have fun

I'm sorting through my clothes for my trip and pulled a couple things that I had worn the day Rick died. I don't want to wear that for this trip, it took a year for me to get them out of the hamper. I feel like the memories would come back too strong and would trigger too many emotions. I guess I'll have to go shopping.

3/27/2012 – I feel very isolated and alone I have no one to share my feelings with. I had my work review today, it's not a big deal but Rick and I would always discuss my objectives for the coming year. He would give me feedback and ideas on what to write for improvements and goals. I sat and chatted with my manager and told him the review used to mean more to me. I'm grateful to have a job, I said, but in the scheme of things it seems so secondary to my life. I'll be productive but my heart or energy is not in it. As I read this, it seems so trivial, yet it's just another reminder I'm on my own.

I've made a project of gathering all the photos of Rick and me. So far I've made an online video, a book from a photo site, I made a photo montage movie to Tina Turner - The Best, and I've downloaded every photo onto a CD. I'm obsessed with keeping these memories; I can't get enough of them. I'm holding on so tight, I don't want anything to be forgotten. I'm digging out all our older photos and taking pictures with my digital camera and uploading to my computer, all so I can make another photo book. I'm so afraid of it all slipping away, that I won't remember him unless I look at the pictures. It makes him seem so alive.

3/28/2012 – Happy Birthday My Love. Enjoy the sweet memories of life. I hope you can hear and feel all the love and laughter coming your way today. Good stories shared, tears cried, a smile curls my lips and my heart aches. Sending you Bunny kisses and hugs out to the universe. May they take flight and bring my love to you.

4/1/2012 – April Fool!!! No it is reality, not a cruel joke….or is it?

I spent the morning sorting through Rick's clothes to give to charity, 60 pieces to be exact; I counted them for a school having a fundraiser. 60 shirts and pants, I neatly folded each one and there is still more to go through. It was a little easier this time until I came across one bag that had some clothes in it. I thought it was something I had started packing up and forgot about until I opened it, that familiar swell of panic came over me. These are the clothes from Rick's suitcase. I had unpacked them and put everything into a plastic bag, tucked it into the closet and forgot about it. I was overcome with emotion as I sunk to the floor buried my face into the pile and sat there crying. No! No! No! I cannot give these away, back into the bag they went and that was all I could handle.

4/4/2012 – I had a strange dream - I woke up to the sounds of wind and fans blowing. I crept out of bed and saw all the windows and doors were open and my big house fan had been turned on. I grabbed my phone and called Rick; he answered but did not say anything else. I remember thinking, why isn't he happy to hear from me? I told him I was scared and did not know what to do. He was very calm and said "well, what do you think it means and why would you think someone did this"? I was confused and crying and I said "I didn't do this - did I"? He then said "you can take care of it". I remember being paralyzed with fear and just standing there looking around. I really thought someone was in the house. Suddenly, I woke up and I listened for a moment glanced around and finally went back to sleep. Is there a message there? And why did I need to call him on the phone?

4/5/2012 – that overwhelming sadness came over me again today. I had dinner with Rick's niece last night and we talked about how funny and caring Rick was. We talked about how Rick died and how long it was before the wake and how none of us really grieved together. I feel so sad for them, his nieces and nephews, for not knowing much about Rick and his life with me. Of course they remember him from their younger days but they know nothing of the last 15 years. I told her about our life together and our wonderful love. The moral here is say I love you often and be with the one you love.

When I got home my heart was aching and the sadness felt heavy. I was walking through the house with that I'm lost and I don't know what to do with myself feeling. Heavy sighs. My back is throbbing and feeling so tight. I know a lot of it is from stress and of course not exercising, can't exercise until it feels better. UGH! I just burst into tears; I think the emotions from the night before caught up with me.

I was watching a TV program and there was a woman facing the fact that her husband had died. She was practicing saying - I'm a widow. My tears flowed as I sat there saying it out loud too - I am a widow. Have I said this before? I think Quinn had me say it, I don't remember. I said it out loud, but in my head I was a asking - really? Do you really mean it as you say it? Are they just words to help define your position in life now?

4/7/2012 – Since Rick died I've been faced with many firsts, tough heart wrenching moments, my first night alone, first holidays, our anniversary and birthdays. I faced each one and whatever emotions came with it. Now this is the first vacation on my own. It is a joyous, fun time for me to regroup yet I'm nervous. I been experiencing highs and lows all week and I burst into tears this morning, one week from today I'm leaving for Cabo. I'm looking forward to relaxing in the sun yet I feel guilty. I deserve to enjoy myself, yet I can't completely shake the nagging feeling that I'm leaving Ricky behind. I'm taking some of his ashes with me and I made a plan of where I want to scatter them. This trip will be a mixed bag of emotions. I've ridden that roller-coaster the last 14 months, I survived, and I buckled up and let the ride take me. Most of it I rode with eyes squeezed shut and hands clenching the safety bar. It's time for eyes wide open and throw those arms up as the ride reaches its peak and takes the plunge. I can't control how or when I'll feel these emotions but I can accept and embrace each moment. This is me living my life now, as I would say - living it out loud. Rick loved my spirit; my heart may be bruised and broken but never my spirit.

I talked with Patty and told her how stressed and nervous I've been. She replied, you're taking Rick with you and he wanted to go! She's right; he did want to go back to Cabo San Lucas this year. Glad I talked with her, feeling calmer now.

4/8/2012 – Happy Easter! I decided to spend the day alone, my back is aching plus I need to get some packing finished. I got up very early today, been sorting clothes for the trip, cleaned house and it is only 3:30. I'm bored! The sun is shining, but it's too cold to be outside now I feel like napping. As you know I've been feeling very nervous and guilty about this trip. I got Chinese takeout today and when I opened my fortune cookie this was the message 'find release from your cares and have a good time'. It was the right message at the right time.

4/10/2012 – I keep having very bizarre dreams. Last night I dreamed my sister Patty fell off a porch. I watched her fall and she landed in the garden and the dream just ends - I had no idea what happened. I called her today just to tell her to be careful. How bizarre! I keep trying to find the meaning in these weird dreams, just my mind on overdrive.

4/10/2012

SHELTERED

Angry sullen torn from an idyllic life

Standing together hand in hand I was sheltered from the storms around me

Thrust now into chaos – mayhem –

forced to face the jaws and claws of the world

Spoiled yes – childlike no not ignorant – worldly wise

Soft exterior – hardened insides legs strong – back stiffened

Braced against the onslaught   the petty   the ugly the truths of the world

Barred now for me to see   pity – the blindness was bliss

4/11/2012 – So many thoughts and emotions are coming up, a combination of nerves and excitement. Nervous because I can't control how I will react on this trip. I feel angry and cheated; Rick should be joining me, we should be enjoying Cabo together. The guilty feelings are still creeping in, would Rick be thinking – Bunny, how could you go someplace so special to us? Or is he saying - Bunny you go and have a great time I'll be walking right beside you? People tell me Rick would be proud, this is a huge step in my recovery. I know it in my head but my heart is scared to experience this on my own. I'll have great support from Cindy and Nick. Remember to balance pain and pleasure and don't be a downer. This trip is not all about you and Rick, everyone else is also on vacation. I'm bringing his ashes, I will have a special day and time to have my moment with the ocean and scatter his ashes with nature. The excitement is there, I'm anxious to get back to see Cabo again.

4/11/2012

MY "TAKE ON" LIFE

You thought you could beat me - you played on my fears

You took me down and watched me struggle - the rivers I could fill

With the flow of my tears - each time I rose up and took you on

gaining strength And growing strong

you tested my will you shook my core - I stood and took it

And asked for more - you thought I would fail I'd run and hide

Did I surprise you with my stubborn pride

I've stood on a mountain – I've run through the fields

I've taken on life – and whatever it deals

You can't keep me down – you won't hold me back

I'll take on life – and forever fight back

The weight of the world seemed to wear me down

Even I had doubts that I could go on

each time I thought it was my darkest hour

A sliver of sun would brighten a corner

for a moment in time the weight had lifted

Through every window the sunshine fell - no longer was I living in hell

Once again you've taken me down - the world is bleak my sunshine gone

I won't give up I won't be weak - I'll keep on fighting I must go on

You thought you could beat me - on my knees I would fall

You thought I'd give up - but here I am standing tall

I've stood on a mountain – I've run through the fields

I've taken on life – and whatever it deals

You can't keep me down – you won't hold me back

I'll take on life – and forever fight back

Again I stand strong and proud - as Ricky taught me living my life out loud

With all the sadness you've brought into my life

I still had the joy of being his wife

What plans do you have for my future years

I've already faced the worst of my fears

You've tried it all you put me to the test

What I got to experience was simply the best

Nothing now can take that away - even with death the memories remain

In my darkest hours I'll reach back in time

and remember the love that once was mine

I've stood on a mountain – I've run through the fields

I've taken on life – and whatever it deals

You can't keep me down – you won't hold me back

I'll take on life – and forever fight back

4/14/2012 – Well, I'm on the plane heading for Cabo, no tears and no fears. We called Patty before boarding and sang Happy Birthday to her and she said to me "no guilt Jan, just enjoy yourself and have fun".

4/15/2012 – It's 8:45am and I already walked the beach. I'm enjoying my coffee and the spectacular view. The vendors are lining up their goods and the jet skis had been taken out into the water inviting someone, anyone to take a thrill ride. Our first day flew by so fast I don't think I even realized I was in Mexico until this morning. Yesterday was a blur, it felt like I was just hanging with friends and I would be heading home soon. As I look out at the water, I see a paddle boarder navigating the early morning swells and then I know - I'm in Cabo. My toes are finally in the sand and I let the water wash over my feet and I feel the energy and power of the ocean. I scattered some of Rick's ashes in front of our beach. As a wave washed them away, I told him to rejoin that energy and wash back over me. As I turned to walk away a wave came up and slapped me on the butt I turned and said "Ricky you just had to do that".

We have had lots of laughs on our first full day, and I think I've had more to drink in 24 hours then the last three months. I was just standing on my balcony and wishing Ricky was standing here with me.

4/17/2012 – I've been up to watch the sunrise every morning and then walking the beach. I'm enjoying this alone time watching the boats and listening to the waves. We've been busy, went into town and we had to have a drink at Cabo Wabo. Tonight during dinner the song "The Best" came on, my hello message from Rick. Miss you my Darling!

4/18/2012 – today Cindy and I went to Sunset Beach Resort, where Rick and I had stayed our last visit. My destination was clear, there is an outcropping of rocks and I knew that is where I wanted to scatter Rick's ashes. The waves were fierce and unpredictable, one minute breaking right at the shore the next trying to take us with them. Cindy took some pictures as I scattered the ashes all around me in the sand. I turned toward the water, blew him a kiss and told him to join his favorite ocean. The timing was perfect, as I stood in the wash of the wave another came up higher and swept the ashes into the ocean. Cindy and I stood for a moment with tears and our eyes and yelled out - goodbye Ricky. We walked the entire beach about 2 miles, memories of Rick and I on that beach filled every step. Later we went up to the sky pool looking out over the ocean from way atop the property.

Today was a real adventure, things I said I would never do or I have a fear of, I did today. I actually ventured into the water and was letting the waves hit me. I'm sure it doesn't sound like a big deal to you but it is for me with my fear of water. Later I climbed into a water taxi, or I should say, Nick dumped me in, and we sped across the water to the marina, next stop the Jungle boat booze cruise. I have seen this boat before and swore I would never go on it, well, never say never. Nick booked it for our sunset cruise and I really wanted to see the sunset and the arch. It was a crazy ride with a lot of partying people, but I ended up enjoying it especially watching Cindy dance with crew members. I spent some time on my own at the front of the boat just watching the sunset over the resorts. All and all it was a good time.

4/21/2012 – It's our last morning and I'm up very early. I've gotten in some long walks, a massage on the beach, some alone time at my favorite restaurant and even ventured into the water this week. I decided to walk around the two resorts one last time; I want the sound of the ocean imbedded into my brain and the beauty of the morning sky, water and rock formation stored in my mind's eye. Being here without Rick was tough, so many memories yet now I'm making my own. This place meant so much to us, on our honeymoon we tasted all Cabo had to offer, her delicious food, fine wine and beautiful spirit. We left a piece of our hearts here then and when we came back in 2009. The mystery of the ocean and the night sky kept us more than occupied, with whale watching, shooting stars and crashing waves we fell permanently in love with Cabo. We vowed to come back in 2012 and I kept that vow. I stood on the shore of the Pacific, waves crashing with the pull of energy, the stark beauty of Sunset Beach and there I scattered Rick's ashes into the sea, wind and water. He now has become part of what we loved, to join the beauty and energy of Cabo, the sea of Cortez and the Pacific Ocean and I know I'll be back. The draw of the ocean is so powerful even though I don't go in, just to feel it on my feet is enough. Watching and listening gives me enough of its power to fill me and stay with me until the next time. Rick's energy is now merged within that power and I will go back again and again and let it surround me. I had a little bit of ashes left, so I walked into the water in front of our hotel and scattered them. The water was so clear and I watched as they were washed back into the sea, as the waves crashed over my feet up onto my calves I thought of it as a hug from Rick. Goodbye for now.

4/24/2012 – Sometimes, when I hide in one room I think the reality of what's really going on can't reach me.

4/28/2012 – I still can't figure out how to manage my time. Rick and I were so good together taking care of each other and the house. We split our weekends into leisure time, chores, cooking and time together. He always knew exactly what he wanted to accomplish and still have plenty of time for us. I tend to start one thing, wander off to another, and then I easily get distracted not finishing anything. It's almost noon I was up around 7:00 AM, started sorting laundry, decided to look for garage sale items, then I saw the vacuum and started to clean the basement. I'm back to my grocery list again which I started 2 hours ago. Eventually I ended up under the basement stairs sorting through boxes of rocks and shells that Rick had collected over the years. I got a good laugh remembering Ricky bringing home each of them year after year from every trip we've been on. I guess I'm off to buy groceries if I can decide what I want. One of these days I will get more organized.

4/30/2012 - Quinn has asked me - where do I think of Rick is? Is he all around me and can I talk to him anywhere and anytime? I like to think he's all around me and when I have something to say I just say it out loud or ask questions. While I was on vacation, I realized the only place that I have these out loud conversations with him is in our home. The whole time I was gone it was more like thoughts or quick statements, for example I'd say 'Ricky walk with me along the beach' or 'please keep me keep me safe'. And as soon as I got home I actually sat and talked with him telling him my thoughts, all about the trip and I even cried. I was so preoccupied on vacation; I didn't need to have all these talks with him or maybe because I wasn't alone. It just feels different here when I'm looking at the urn, I have a focal point when talking out loud. He is in my heart and mind always; I guess when I'm out, busy doing whatever, I'm not focused on my thoughts and the need to talk them out with Ricky. Yet I still can't leave the house without saying goodbye or I have to be in the same room as the urn when I need to talk to him.

I almost forgot I had another lost jewelry incident. For some reason, I took the necklace that has Rick's ashes in it with me to Cabo. Once I got there I put it away and never thought of it again until I got home. I thought I lost it, I searched everywhere for it, I even called the airport and the hotel looking for it. How could I have been so careless! I cried and told Ricky I'm so sorry I lost the locket in Mexico. I went about my day and I was really pissed off. Later, as I was taking my clothes out of the dryer, the locket literally shot out and landed at my feet. I could not believe it once again Ricky heard me and answered my plea.

5/3/2012 –A widow, grieving, still filled with sadness, holding onto memories, that's me that's the definition of who I am now. Not ready, unwilling to let go - to move on. I keep hearing - start a new life. Start how? For 14 years I had a purpose, a goal, I was the love of Rick's life and he mine. Yes, I had my own personality, I still do. But, my life was fixed, set in stone, I was the other half and together we were complete. All clichés - yet true. So, when I'm ready and willing, I'll find who I am and what my purpose is now. Until then - I settle into the dark comfort of sorrow.

5/5/2012 – I carry on the same routine of saying good morning, goodnight, goodbye and kissing you (the urn) to keep my memories of you. I talk to and kiss the urn because I'm so afraid the memories will disappear and just like your physical self be gone forever. I'm so superstitious about my routine, I won't deviate from it. I've tried to leave without a kiss or saying goodbye; I just come back in and do it anyway. It was weird on vacation without having something tangible to touch and see. I want to believe your presence is all around me. If I stay quiet and really open my mind, I imagine you here trying to embrace me. There are times I'm not sure at all, but I'm afraid to stop talking to and touching the urn. If there's a chance at all that you can hear me, feel me, reaching out to you, I don't want to lose that.

5/6/2012 – Annie will be one year old in a few days. Having Erin back in Chicago, and her mom Linda visiting every month, was such a good distraction for me. Spending time with them and watching Annie grow has helped me find my smile again. I have a purpose and a reason to share my love.

ANNIE MY ANGEL–

In the days of my deepest despair came an angel so pure and fair

My darkest hours were now filled with light

came a little angel so cute and bright

Little Annie on this day was born one look at her face and this I knew

My sorrow forgotten my heart beat anew

she cuddled and crawled her way into my life

Her auntie could make her squeal with delight

she's walking now really on her way

Just waiting for the day she calls out my name

a beauty she'll be of that I'm sure

She's only one with so much in front of her I'll be there each and every step

I'll cherish her everyday her auntie will always love her

More than words could ever say oh little Annie angel that you are

Heaven smiled upon me the day that you were born - My love to you always
- Auntie Jan (TiTi)

5/7/2012 - I went to Gloria's for dinner, being around any of the Bersani family is like an extension of Rick. Their love is like a big, warm, constant embrace, unconditional and from the heart. Rick picked up some very good habits from hanging with this family so much.

5/10/2012 - Sometimes our common sense leaves us when we're sick. You can't stop running to the bathroom and your stomach is completely wrenched and you're wondering "hmmm wonder if I should call the doctor, is this flu or a stomach virus"? I actually called the emergency room and asked this question without much help. Told me to keep an eye on fever and stay hydrated, if you get worse then call your doctor. How much worse?? After several bouts in the bathroom, fever of 101, so weak I can barely stand and real bizarre dreams, exactly when do you call the doctor? Stay hydrated?! I can barely stay awake long enough to take my temp, how can I drink enough water. I fell asleep with the thermometer in my mouth! I have barely moved and unable to keep my eyes open for 24 hours; I literally lost one whole day. Feels like my insides are being gnawed apart, but, I'll wait it out to see how I am later. UGH! Ricky would have bundled me up and gotten me in to see someone, flu or not someone better check on his Bunny. I miss him rubbing my fevered head and upset tummy, bringing me soup and tea. Even though it didn't heal, it was very comforting. He would have been at my side making sure I had everything I needed. Maybe I'll call the doctor if I get worse…ha!

5/12/2012 - Happy Anniversary my Darling - it would be 11 years; my heart and soul still belong to you. I made a little video montage today keeping our memories alive and sharing that wonderful smile and beautiful eyes with everyone. Love you my Big Dog miss you so much. Today is Annie's first birthday party, so I'll be with my sweet angel girl today. I wish it was just you and I celebrating our anniversary, but I know you're with me especially today. Kiss – Kiss – Kiss – oh, how my heart is aching right now.

5/13/2012 - With today being mother's day, I've been thinking about my mom. For the first time I'm realizing just how strong she was. When my dad died she was only 48 with two girls still living at home. She suffered, we all saw it, but she managed through it. She went back to work fulltime and eventually met her second husband, he too died and she went on alone, I don't even think she was 60 yet. She stayed active, worked fulltime and had good social life; she danced and even played volleyball. She never stayed still; she was always on the go. When she died she was on her way to hit all the stores for the senior discounts and play her lottery tickets. How did I become so lazy? It's not in my DNA both of my sisters are good at getting things done. We all like to relax but I do take advantage, especially a nice warm day, sunshine and the outdoors beckoning me. In fact it's calling me right now! I miss you Mom, wishing you were here to talk with, you of all people would understand my sorrow. I could also use some of your insight and your strength. Happy Mother's Day Mom.

5/15/2012 - When Quinn and I were talking, he pointed out that I often question if what I do at home with the urn is "normal". You know, I kiss it, I hug it and I talk to it and carry it into different rooms. I hear myself telling someone I do these things and wonder if they think I'm crazy. I'm the crazy widow lady sitting with an urn carrying on conversations. I'm content and it's how I cope. These little habits comfort me and I feel closer to Ricky. So I guess the answer is, I don't care what anyone else thinks, it make me feel better.

5/17/2012 – Today is a beautiful Spring day and I feel the familiar sting of tears as I drive into our subdivision and come around the corner. I can picture Rick sitting on the patio, getting sun on his face patiently waiting for me to join him. He'd hear me come in and yell 'Hi Honey, I'm out here'. I'd give anything to hear that one more time.

5/19/2012 – I just watched some of our videos again. It's getting harder for me to hear your voice in my mind. Remembering how you said my name, the different tones in your voice and your sense of humor. I'm so lucky to not only have so many photos of you but also video of you and your voice. I sit with my eyes closed and listen as you're giving us a tour of the resort we stayed at. That voice lifted me every morning with your daily phone call, telling me good morning darling - I love you. Being able to hear you and watch you swim helps keep you alive in my mind. It also makes my heart ache for you and again I cry.

5/28/2012 - Another unofficial start to summer weekend spent without Rick. I felt so lost this morning. Our day would have been - coffee on the patio before the sun gets too hot, some quiet time together and probably Rick barbecuing enough to last the week. I did manage to sit out and have some early morning coffee. Weekends are difficult enough for me, but the long weekends drag on. At least I spent part of this weekend with Erin and my little Annie. I love the time off but hate the alone time, everyone has plans and I'm home feeling sorry for myself.

I had a talk with Ricky - I asked 'when is it time to start thinking of meeting someone'. I guess since I asked the question I must be thinking about it. I'm not really looking for romance or love; even saying that makes me cringe. It would be nice to have someone with common interests to hang out with, no commitment just mutual interests, like concerts, street fairs and walking around the city. Everyone said it's what Rick would want; he wants you to be happy. I went straight to the source and I asked for myself, now if it's meant to be, someone will pop into my life.

5/29/2012 - Oh my God Rick! I miss you! I've been on the verge of tears since yesterday. I am so lonely and bored. Oh, how you filled my days, my life. I come home, I don't smile, laugh or talk; except the occasional comments I make to you. Our home was filled with laughing and conversation, I don't like the quiet, and I don't think I'll ever get used to it. Also, I know I talked to you about when should I start meeting someone, my stomach has been jumpy all day and the thought of it scares me to death. Plus, how can I, I'm still so wrapped in our memories I don't know if I would let anyone get close to me. The thought of being intimate in anyway makes me nauseous and I have tears in my eyes right now. I feel guilty, scared and sick all at the same time. What do I do?? Am I destined to be alone? Either way it goes, I'm terrified at spending my life alone or starting a new relationship. I just need to figure out how to start my new life alone first. No one could ever replace you or come close. I would not want anyone to try. But, how do I not compare, that's easy – nobody compares to you. You're simply the best, better than all the rest, and I was so lucky to have had you in my life.

6/2/2012 - Staying busy, I hate being home. Visits with my sisters, lunch with friends, hanging at Erin's, anything to not be home alone. Hours drift by, and I'm unaware. I wonder out loud "where did the day go?" I've done nothing but sit at the computer or stare at the TV. Did I eat?? I don't think so. Time drags on and that's when I long for Ricky. Summer month's days start early and go on forever, for me, it's just torture, I want the day to end, yet sleep does not come easy. We loved the warm months, couldn't wait to be outside. I sit in the house and can't yet enjoy our yard.

6/3/2012

LONELY DAYS

Lonely days   the sun shines   but I don't feel the warmth

Lonely nights   the stars shine   but I only see dark

I smile and there are still tears in my eyes

I laugh - yet my heart is breaking   I am a Zombie in this world

I move through the days and nights - unseen - unheard - unnoticed

My voice silent   my thoughts unknown

A secret world - others have no need no desire to share

Quietly I suffer   my face a mask to the world   I am no one   alone I cry

6/6/2012 – So I'm joking with Dr. Tom about me being the crazy old widow lady that never comes out of the house, wearing a ratty old housecoat or sweats, hair is all matted, talking to myself all hunched over with gnarly nails. I said that's me in a few years! Sometimes I feel like I'll just wither away. He said - nope that is not you ever- some days I wonder.

Nothing seems any easier, for over a year I've been feeling and thinking the same way. How could this have happened? This sucks! What is life without Ricky? - Bored, empty and lonely.

As I pulled into the garage, I swore the inside door opened and then shut quickly. My heart leapt, I gripped the steering wheel and just sat staring at the door willing into open again. You see, Rick used to greet me at that door. If he was in the kitchen and heard me coming, he'd run to open the entry door, pop his head out, smile at me and close the door again. He'd then reopen it throw me a kiss or sometimes he would moon me. Always making me laugh and always there to welcome me home. So in that brief moment I thought he was standing there, maybe he was just letting me know he's still around. Sometimes that hurts even more, thinking, that somehow he knows I'm here and he watches over me and that I can never see, touch or hear him again.

6/7/2012 – Living alone you find out very quickly you're not perfect. You know, all those nitpicky things you would point out to your spouse, guess what - you do them too. I too, drip water on the floor and then I step and it, nobody to blame but me. Yes, Rick always dripped water, made crumbs or broke the TV remote. I would roll my eyes; fix the remote, clean up the crumbs or wipe up the water, now I'm doing the exact same thing for myself. I'd give anything to step in those water drips or hear Rick yell 'Bunny the remote won't work'. It just makes me miss him more thinking of all these little things.

6/13/2012 - It has been a month since I've seen Quinn, I thought it would be easy that I wouldn't need to talk to him as often. Wrong! I have a lot of pent up feelings and I realized this process could go on forever. I want to hold onto Rick so tight yet I want to know what is next for me, but I stay frozen, paralyzed unable to make any decisions. I become frustrated and sad at the same time. I kept saying "it's almost 18 months" and Quinn would say "it's only 18 months you still have a lot to go through". I need to stay in the moment more, be mindful of the times I slip into a time lapse. Hours go by and I lose track of time, he would like to see me structure my weekends more. Try to eat at the appropriate times be more healthy and try to work in some walks. He's right, his work with me and Dr. Toms work do go hand in hand. They say healthy mind healthy body, most days I say - who cares.

6/17/2012 - When you're married, free time is harder to come by and it always seems like friends are doing something or going someplace. How many times have you said 'Oh I wish I could go on that weekend trip too' or 'my time is so limited, I need to choose carefully - maybe next time. In my case, I enjoyed my time with Rick, but even I wished for free time a few hours on weekends. Now I have all the free time - 24 hours a day. And all those things other people are doing that I thought I was missing out on, well that's only equal to once or twice a year. All those other days and hours are filled with nothing. If you think you're missing out on something, it's probably one out of all the thousands of hours in your life. So, now I try to fill all that time and I hear from everyone else, 'oh, I wish I could join you but I'm busy or the family and I are busy. So be careful when you wish for more of your own time you could actually hate the results. I would take back every second

I insisted on watching TV because I just couldn't miss an episode, so I could have that time back with Rick.

Happy father's day daddy! I been thinking of you all day and all the things you've missed in our lives - miss you.

6/18/2012 - I spent time this weekend with my family and some extended family. I took that opportunity to talk with them all about how things are still very tough for me and how my heart still aches. Erin and Linda said it best "you always smile and seem OK and we forget that you're still healing". Erin said "I never want to bring up Rick because you seem happy and I don't want to say something to make you sad". I told them I'm sad every day, it doesn't matter how I'm feeling, doing or how I look; there is sadness deep inside of me. Yes, Annie makes me laugh and smile yet I'm still sad that she'll never know Rick. It felt good to be able to share with everyone that I still have so much pain; I'm always so concerned about making others uncomfortable that sometimes I hide my feelings. I also talked with Rick's cousins and my sisters.

6/24/2012 - I took Quinn's advice and made my weekend more constructive. I ran my errands, I ate healthy, I even got a walk in and my time seemed more organized. He was right, it helped to break up my day into segments and I did not feel as chaotic and scattered, I actually feel calm.

6/25/2012 – There are triggers that either bring up a memory or just remind me of Rick and I can't help crying. Jason Mraz song - I Won't Give Up – makes me cry so much. Every time I hear it the tears just start streaming. Bon Jovi, Livin on a Prayer, reminds me of Rick and me dancing at the end of a wedding. The two of us dancing and singing at the top of our lungs and Rick jumping up and down, just rocking out. I can still see his face, the way he would pucker his mouth and suck in his cheeks, putting on his dancing face. I heard it on the way home tonight and at first I was smiling the next thing I knew, I was crying, happens every time. I find myself searching for these songs on the radio or looking them up on you tube, just to feel that emotion. I play them over and over crying and hitting replay.

6/26/2012

THUNDER CRASHES IN

Who do I run to when the thunder crashes in

Who do I lean on when my world is upside down

Who will hold me up when my body grows weary

Who do I turn to with all the questions in my mind

I will be strong I will be brave - Stand up tall and find my way

Embrace the fear or it holds you down - With eyes wide open I'll follow my heart

Who will calm me and soothe my fears

Who will save me when the walls are closing in

Who will guide me when I know not where to turn –

Who will shelter me against the winds

I will be strong I will be brave - Stand up tall and find my way

The answers are out there this I believe - My path will be bright I'll trust where it leads

6/28/2012 – Moving forward does not mean I'm leaving Rick behind

6/29/2012 – Everything I do in a day, I compare to what or how Rick and I would do it. This is my thought process from the time I get up until I go to bed. I catch myself looking at the clock and thinking 'Rick would be calling me now' or 'he should be walking in the door any moment'. Whatever the moment, it has a memory of Rick attached. My drive home is filled with smiles and memories of Rick out on the patio or waiting for me at the door.

We would chat about our day, and of course, catch up on political news. I so miss those moments and time is so empty now. I turned to Rick for everything, his advice and his wonderful knowledge, whether it was what I made for dinner or what our weekend would be. Rick knew my heart and soul and I put all my faith and trust into him. Now, I need to trust me, have faith in me. Trust that I can see the truth. Trust who I can turn to and who will not allow me to fall. Trust – that's the key. It took months for me to let Rick fully into my life. Now, my guard is up and I'm at my most vulnerable state. I need people, yet, who can I truly trust??

7/3/2012 – A small group of Osgood cousins went to the Sox game, 96 degrees but we're having a blast. Sox won 19 to 2!

7/4/2012 –Happy Birthday America! Too hot to do much, I sat out early then headed to the mall to get out of the 100 degree temps. I feel so worn out.

I went to the bridge on Beverly Road to watch the fireworks. We did this since we moved out here; we could see all the suburbs around us and the best part, we were alone. As I turned the corner, I was shocked to see hundreds of people lining the bridge. Found out our town merged with two others and the fireworks were now right across the expressway. One more thing in my life that has changed, this is no longer "our spot".

7/6/2012 – No relief from the heat, I'm down for the count, must be dehydrated.

I saw an interesting quotes today "I am not a victim, I know suffering but I'm still standing. Self pity is an excuse to do nothing. To seek sympathy for pity sake is to seek affirmation of the choice to do nothing. I am empowered by the spirit and support of meaningful experience and I transform with silent resilience"

Interesting that I had said to Quinn that I want to 'hang on' to the pain and I want everyone to still mourn with me. That I want to feel the pain and if I don't, I'm leaving Rick behind. We talked about having more positive thoughts and about moving forward in my life. He wanted me to write something in a positive light and not in the fear of forgetting Rick. That's why I wrote last week 'moving forward does not mean I'm leaving Rick behind'. I guess the universe and Rick are sending me back the same message.

7/7/2012 - Going to see all the Bersani's for 4th of July celebration, looking forward to the hugs, kisses, good conversation and of course all the good food.

I will open my mind and heart to new adventures and experiences. All will be OK, enjoy my days, and love myself and the life in front of me. Quinn and I also talked about my defeatist attitude. I said - even when I see Dr. Tom, I go in thinking my results are going to be so bad he will lecture me. It's another way that I have of hanging onto pain and grief. Keeping others involved in my struggle and looking for the affirmation that it's still OK to suffer and stay where I am. Neither Tom nor Quinn are supporting me and letting me get away with this anymore. Yes, I will always have the pain of losing Rick yet I need to take care of me. No more sitting still!

It seems after I write these words of positive thoughts and affirmations of moving forward, several hours later the floodgates open. Tears are streaming and I'm crying over the loss of you, losing what we had and what could be, crying over you losing the chance to do so much more. I'm crying over the thought that I could possibly move forward and be happy, or even be happy with someone else. I want we had and I only want it with you! I don't care if everyone thinks it's OK to be out, to be social. I know it's OK but I want us back. It's impossible, I know it, yet my heart aches for it. I'm afraid; afraid of failing or being rejected yet I'm afraid of being alone. That is the problem. Stagnant water will fill with poison and die. I'm a free spirit and need to run fresh and free. I'm certain I do not want to die, even for the chance I'll be with Ricky, so much else to be lost.

7/8/2012 - Everyone wants to assure me it's OK to move on and find out what's out there, see what's next for Jan. I was with all the Cousins last night, like I always said, being with them is one long special hug. I feel so lifted from their energy. Joe and Ted are the patriarchs of the family, I love and respect them both and I had a great conversation with them. I walked away so uplifted and so supported from them both. They both assured me Rick would be happy to see me continue into the next phase of my life. Ted, gracious as he always is, had wonderful memories of Rick and I as a couple. We talked of the tragic loss to all of us and how Rick made everyone laugh and smile. He said it would make them all happy to see me move on and live out my life, be happy, Rick would want that. Thanks to Ted and Joe, love you both.

7/15/2012 – I had a nice leisure morning getting ready to drive out to Lake Geneva to stay at the time share. The last time I was up here was July 2009 for my birthday. I have many fond memories it's time to make new ones. Cindy and Deb met me and are spending the night to celebrate my birthday. We had a great day at the pool and then off to dinner in town. We took a long walk and back to our room for a nightcap they sang happy birthday to me at midnight.

7/16/212 - Happy birthday to me! Another day spent that the pool and a little power shopping. Before I knew it was time for them to go home. My best laid plans have gone astray; I planned on having my birthday dinner at our favorite restaurant here at the resort. Rick and I had many fond memories and a couple birthday celebrations at this restaurant, but, they're closed so now what. I do not have a backup plan and I'm sitting in my beautiful room feeling sorry for myself. I made myself a cocktail, relaxed a little bit and decided to go to dinner at the café. So here I am sitting in a restaurant having dinner alone on my birthday, thank God for that view. I made it through just fine, nobody stared at me and I did not feel self conscious. Tomorrow night I'll go to Brissago and I'll celebrate. It's a beautiful evening and I decided to take a walk. Rick and I always made a point of walking this path, and we'd

127

sit in the Adirondack chairs at the top of the hillside overlooking the golf course. I decided to scatter some of Rick's ashes here, it's the perfect spot for Rick's spirit, the hawks soaring over the field and a family of geese and ducks were swimming on the lake. A couple women saw me sitting and asked if I wanted my picture taken, which I thought was odd. I said no that's OK; I have plenty of pictures from the past when my husband and I came up here. She insisted and said 'no I think you'd love to have a picture taken' so I gave her my camera and she took a couple pictures of me. Later, as I walked away I cried, I cried for the memories and the fact that I'm making new ones without Rick. I know he's here with me I feel him all around me. I have not been sad or afraid up here on my own, just a little lonely and missing conversation. The view and all the activities around me are a good distraction and keep me company.

7/17/2012 – I spent the day at the pool, felt so relaxed today reading, people watching and even going into the water. Back in the room getting ready for dinner, I really noticed the quiet.

As I was seated at my table for dinner, I was greeted with several happy birthday wishes and rose petals on the table. It's a bit intimidating sitting alone, you never know where to look, again thank God for the view. Every table is full with lots of conversation around me; this is when I feel lonely. As darkness falls the view is obscured and the room begins to feel smaller. I'm aware of all the couples around me and all the conversations, now I'm more focused on sitting alone. I drink my wine and find myself eavesdropping, one couple is planning their wedding, and a couple by the window reminds me of Rick and me. She gives him a bite of her food, they try each other's wine, and they hold hands and kiss. I have a lump in my throat and for a moment my eyes fight back the tears, instead I smile remembering how happy we were and wishing these couples the same. And now stuffed to the gills and just a little lightheaded from two glasses of wine, I run into the couple that was by the window as I'm leaving. They're celebrating 20 years of marriage and turning 50. I tell them that they remind me of us and all the wonderful memories we made up here and I wish them well. Back in my room there's no sadness no tears, I feel calm and satisfied. It sounds weird but the night turned out how I imagined and I feel good about it. It was a nice birthday celebration now off to bed.

7/18/2012 - I'm sitting at the pool at 7:00 AM, it's a peaceful lovely morning. Sitting here overlooking the rolling landscape bring such peace to me. The sky seems endless and I watch a hawk scout his meal. Being in a nature setting really calms my soul.

After I checked out, I drove into town to walk the lake path. After about a mile I found a beautiful spot where the path curved, weeping willows and a few other trees bent out over the water. This is the perfect spot to scatter more ashes. It was breezy and they blew along the tree line into the water and onto the path. I'll easily recognize this spot and remember Rick's spirit is here and all the times we walked together. He'll be here in nature, watching for me, I know he'll keep me safe anytime I take this walk.

So, the weekend is over and, dare I say it, I had a wonderful time. I laughed, I cried, I ate way too much but mostly I was relaxed and at ease. A few moments here and there made me self conscious, but most of the time I enjoyed myself. I thought of Rick the whole time, yet not in a sad or depressed way although I missed him very much, especially at dinner. The one thing I realized, I did not feel guilty, I felt as if I deserved every minute soaking up the sun, having a good laugh and enjoying everyone and everything around me. I felt the energy, as if I was being pushed into going to dinner and being by the pool. I felt confident and strong, ready to take on my next adventure - bring it on universe. I can see the light and I'm ready to shine again. My crawl has turned to a stumble and I'm ready to walk tall.

7/20/2012 – My heart is breaking today, 71 people shot and 12 have died in Colorado. Innocent people sitting in a movie theater, watching the new Batman movie, the gunman walked in and just started shooting. How fragile life is, you start your day taking for granted you'll be home with your loved ones, then you're gone in a blink of an eye.

7/28/2012 - Sometimes I feel as if I blank out long spaces of time. I go through the routine of going to the office, heading home, watching TV and time for bed, next thing I know many days have passed. My thoughts seem to be so mundane right now, what to wear, what should I take for lunch, blah, blah, blah. My days are the same as they always were; the huge gap is the time I spent with Rick. I just need something to look forward to, not necessarily every day, just a new purpose and new focus. I was looking at some college courses for creative writing, who knows what could happen.

I'm pulling myself and so many directions I don't know what to do next. I want to get my journal typed and published and my poems put into songs. I'm scared, scared of making the wrong choice and scared of failure. I'm coming up with ideas, deciding if I want to follow through and deciding if it's the right thing for me. I'm making all the decisions in my life, Rick was always my voice of reason, my sounding board, just one more thing I need to learn on my own to trust my choices and use my intuition. Everyone seems to think it's a great idea to put my journal into a book and have my poems turned into music. It gives me confidence to go forward, just not sure how or where to start.

I had a couple glasses of wine and fell asleep in the big chair, another way for me to lose track of time. I'm sure I'll pay for this tomorrow!

7/29/2012 - I just returned from a long walk, I was feeling good and powerful. About 10 minutes from my house, several men were busy working on their landscaping. Suddenly that familiar sickening tightness hit my stomach and my throat closed up. I started to breathe heavy and tried to fight back the panic and pain with no luck, the tears came and now I'm sobbing as I continue to walk past those husbands hard at work. Images of Rick fill my mind; he's sitting in the lawn pulling weeds or turning the mulch around the trees and bushes. My mind has an overload of images and I let out a moan and cry. My pace slows and I'm in no hurry now to get home. That powerful feeling has been replaced with intense sadness and loss. These feelings come so fast, I try to control them but have to give in. I was feeling so full of energy, now I'm left with the same emptiness I've been facing all year. Sunday's Suck! OK, regroup and carry on, this too shall pass. I can miss Rick, feel the pain, embrace it and then move on. I need to do this for me; I've allowed the pain and despair to control me since Rick died. I had to, I would have gone crazy pushing it down, now I'm living with it, recognizing it but not letting it consume me. I am alive and I need to live on. Take in all emotions, filtering out what will destroy who I am, who I will become. I'm not saying I will not mourn for Rick; I do and will continue to mourn my loss, his lost chances in life and the loss of our life. My feelings and love of Rick will never diminish. I'm learning to let the sorrow come over me, yet not wrap me in the cocoon of fear. It's a balancing act, walking the fine line between lost in depression and working with and excepting the emotions.

6:30PM - Mom, I don't know how you managed being alone all those years. I've kept busy most of my day but time still drags on. It's like being in solitary confinement, no human contact for 48 hours. I can pick up the phone and talk, text or e-mail, but it's still lacking the human touch. I want to say I'm sorry to you for any of the times I might have rolled my eyes or said something negative when you asked me to visit you. I get it, I'm now living it. Sometimes I read magazines out loud just to hear my voice and feel like I'm having a conversation. Normal or not it gets me through the silence of a weekend.

7/31/2012 - An observation - I know life lessons are a learning experience, I don't mind them once in awhile, but sometimes they just mess up perfectly good day.

8/4/2012 - We have entered the true hazy lazy days of summer, record temps and sunny dry days. As Chicagoans we look forward to warm weather, the first day over 50°men take to wearing shorts. So far this summer has been brutal the complete opposite of our sub zero winter. Just as you feel trapped in your home in the winter I now feel trapped in my home in the summer. So, instead of enjoying a lovely summer morning I've taken to staying in bed too long. Having the extra daylight, summer is a blessing, you can take extra long walks or sit and read in your lawn chair and not feel as if you're wasting any time. Yet, I'm becoming as hazy and lazy as the days are, instead of gaining strength and energy from the light and the sun I've given in to laziness and boredom. Every day I complain about how tired and achy I am, my clothes are too tight and weight keeps creeping up on me. I have all the knowledge, tools and support yet I can't or won't get moving. Get moving! That seems to be my mantra this year, get moving both mentally and physically. You would think, if you can't wear half of your clothes that would be the motivation you need. Every time I say this is the week I'll start, instead I think I actually gain another pound! As Quinn told me; don't try to analyze every motive or non action just start making the changes needed, I guess I should start listening to his advice. Maybe I need a coach constantly in my face pushing me to be better? Oh wait - that would be me! If I'm not listening to myself then who would I listen to? Open your ears and your mind Jan!

8/10/2012 – I made a big change today, I canceled Rick's cell phone service. It was my last 'connection' to him but it was time. In the first few months after he died I would call his phone just to hear him say his name. His voice is not lost to me I have all the videos that I can listen to. It seems such a small simple thing, yet it felt so big to me. I finally cut free, I should not say finally, it's not like I was held down yet it felt very symbolic that way.

8/12/2012 - I went to a party last night, and a woman who lost her husband right after Rick died was also there. We sat together, asked each other how are you, and talked a bit of the struggle and the loneliness. Two widows, mirrors reflecting back at ourselves. I watched her, as I'm sure she watched me, throughout the night. Gauging just how much she smiles and laughs, is it OK if I laugh and smile too. I see the fear and sadness in her eyes, can she also see mine. I feel relaxed and it seems easy for me to talk to people. As the night goes on we had a few drinks and the mood lightened, we laughed a little louder we even danced and sang. Does she wonder, as I do, is this too much - what are people thinking. Our group pushed us to dance and even karaoke, I'm enjoying myself and wonder if she is too. I've stepped out of my comfort zone and I've moved past caring, no I'm not drunk, I just realize this is fun. She's left the party but I continue on. My laugh and my fun are real and I'm enjoying it, feels good.

8/13/2012

Standing on the edge ready to break free

Standing on the edge afraid of what I'll see

Every step I take leads to a one way street

Standing on the edge I'm ready to be me

8/15/2012

My darling Rick every day I miss you - Every day and every night, at some point, I think of you

I will smile, I will cry, I will remember and I will miss you

8/16/2012 – Happy Birthday Sammie!!

Cindy, Debbie and I walked the Elvis 5k at the lake front tonight. Afterwards we continued walking; we put in over 7 miles. My feet and legs are burning but it feels good.

8/20/2012 - I'm exhausted! I spent the weekend at Erin's. Annie is a ball of nonstop energy, she kept Linda and I on the move. I enjoy her so much, she makes me laugh and act crazy silly. The air and water show was this weekend and we could hear it and see it from the backyard. As the jets were making their practice rounds, right over our heads, it reminded me of the weekend Rick proposed August 20, 1999 it seems a lifetime ago.

I saw Quinn tonight and he asked me if I thought about dating. I didn't know how to answer except to say "well, I've thought of it and I guess I would be open to it, maybe meeting someone with shared interests would be nice". That was quite the answer, yes I think about it because I am lonely and bored, and I just don't think it's a good reason to date. I'm still putting up pictures of Rick and I all around the house and putting together wedding pictures to hang on the wall. I might be lonely and bored but I'm not ready to allow someone to share my heart. I'm so wrapped up in keeping Rick alive it would feel like I'm cheating on him. I might not be crying my eyes out every day, but I miss Rick so much. I want to keep the memories fresh; I want to tell the stories to keep him alive. Still today, as I look at Ricky's photos, it's difficult to think of him as dead. This larger than life personality came into my life and filled every corner, 18 months later I still expect to hear his voice at any moment. In the stillness of the house I listen and I pray I'll hear him whisper my name.

8/27/2012 – It's funny how my memory works, or doesn't. Half the time I can't remember what I did yesterday or what I should be doing today. But, every memory of Rick and I can be played over and over in my mind. Our first date, how he looked at our wedding, every special or even normal everyday moments I can see in my mind. I'll sit sometimes, and like a photo album, I can flip through the years and bring up the images in my head. I can close my eyes and hear our conversations. Rick is embedded in my heart and soul so deep, how can I ever have new memories? I can't imagine sharing that space with someone new. How do I allow someone into my life? Everything reminds me of Rick or something we did together, I don't want to let it go, I don't know how to let it go. I feel sad for me, I'm stuck and I'm the only one that can set me free. Free to do what? I don't know. I just know I can't relive my yesterdays forever and sustain my life, as today is passing me by. I came home tonight and just sat and stared, seeing nothing, just staring and letting my mind wander aimlessly. I sat like that for about twenty minutes. I feel drained with no desire to move, yet, I go to bed and can't sleep. What is going on with me??!

8/28/2012 – Nick and Cindy are in the Bahamas, Nick surprised Cindy and proposed to her. I'm so happy for them, she deserves this. I was so excited I could not sleep!

9/1/2012 – I went to a 70th birthday celebration for Dave, one of Rick's cousins. It was held in a banquet hall and it felt like a wedding reception, there I sat, the single person at the table with couples all around me. There was even a band, I know Rick and I would have danced all night, I only danced once. I've been to several large parties over the past year yet this felt different, it was formal with seating cards and there it was in black and white my name alone. That's when it hit me, my first big function as a single person. Tomorrow we're having a surprise party for Nick and Cindy to celebrate their engagement, so all week my emotions have been all over the place, but I am looking forward to this party.

9/2/2012 - We pulled off the surprise, it's so good see Cindy happy. Although it was hard for me to keep a happy face hearing earlier today Patty and Bill have to move out of their house. I'm so upset by this news yet I want to be happy for Cindy and Nick, so I smile and have a few drinks. At one point I could not fake it anymore, I went to the basement and I cried. I cried for Patty, I cried over Cindy's happiness and yes I cried for the pity of me. I can't help them, and I hate that and I cried for being in this alone. I see Cindy and Nick happy and smiling, hugging and so in love, that was Rick and I just a short time ago. Oh boo-hoo, poor me!

9/6/2012- I've been keeping busy yet I feel so lonely. Ricky I hate this! I getting out of the house as much as possible, I know I can't replace you in any way, I'm just trying to find me again. Tonight I cry…I miss you so much.

9/13/2012 – I ask for guidance from all that watch over me. Show me my path, show me my strength. Rick always saw the beauty in me. Yes, I know he said

I was beautiful, but he also saw it in me. He saw a power deep in me that I just can't seem to find. Help me find who I am, help me find my passion.

9/14/2012 – How many times have I heard the following statement – "it was his time" really!? Do we have a time stamp from inception, use by - or you'll be sorry for the waste. Are we like a carton of milk, left to rot from the inside out? Do you just get tossed away or do you pour yourself into life and nourish those around you. If that's the case then should we all live with wild abandonment? Live for today for tomorrow shall not come. Or, we can make a statement in the world, place your mark on everyone you meet and become unforgettable. Is there a moment, as you take your last breath, to realize which you were? Do we have an 'Oh Shit' moment and think - I wish I would have…… or - that was a great life I have no regrets except how sad it is leaving my loved ones behind.

The other statement I hear "he's in a better place". I take issue with this one, what better place could Rick possibly be but at my side. Being raised Catholic; I know we're all taught of the glory of Heaven. I like to believe we continue on, that there is a Heaven or something celestial. Is it really better to be there than next to the love of your life? Someday my time will be up and I'll find out. In the meantime, I guess I'm somewhere in the middle of "Oh Crap, I wish I could change some of the things from the past, and hey, it's a pretty good life". So I'll continue on, try to keep a positive attitude and make the most of my life. Love deeply, smile and laugh often and dance whenever I feel like it.

9/18/2012 – Linda and I were babysitting Annie the past few days, and she called me Auntie for the first time. What a way to brighten my day!

9/20/2012 – Dr. Quinn and I had a good talk about the reason I'm not taking care of myself, as in, I'm not eating right or exercising. Dr. Tom has been my supporter for several years. It took Rick a little while to get on board with my shakes and all my exercising, I think it took some time away from us and he didn't like it so much at first. I then convinced him it was for us, for me and our health and then he was 100% behind it. Ricky loved me no matter how I looked but he felt as proud as I did at what I accomplished and how good I looked and felt. Since Rick's death, I've fallen into bad eating habits and basically no exercise. The more my mind and heart heal my body just gets worse. I keep saying I don't care but I really do, I put most of the weight I had lost back on, and I feel like crap. 18 months of doing nothing and my body hates me for it. I realize Dr. Tom has become my substitute person for the needy side of me that need to feel like someone has concern and cares about me. If everyone thinks I'm doing OK I'm afraid I'll fade into the background. As time goes on everyone can see I'm healing. "You're doing great Jan" I keep hearing, the funny thing nobody says anything about my weight gain and staying healthy except Dr. Tom. I've replaced all the sympathy and caring I was getting from friends and family with Dr. Tom chastising me every visit, and me promising I'll do better. I walk out and change nothing; it's a way for me to hang onto that need of someone caring about me. He'll sit me down and want to know what is going on with me. Somewhere in my mind this has replaced all the sympathy I was getting. If I start eating right and working out, the caring won't be there, I won't be poor Jan any more. Now I can see this and realize he is still my supporter and he does care, it's not just because I'm suffering, he cares about my health. After being a coach potato all these months it will take some time to get motivated and moving again. One of these days I will find myself.

9/24/2012 – Feeling so disconnected lately, I came home tonight feeling down - just blah. It's difficult to describe, I'm bored and so lonely, yet I did not want to talk to anyone today. I spent time with my sisters over the weekend; even they have so much going on right now. Cindy is packing up her house to move in with Nick and Patty and Bill are moving into Cindy's house. I feel as if I can't talk about myself around them, everyone is so stressed out. Thank God for therapy, although I won't see Quinn for a few weeks. Even Amber and I have not had much time together; she moved and is much farther away now. I feel so isolated and lost, I broke down again, the emotions just well up and the floodgates opened. I just kept crying and asking Ricky "why did you leave me"?! "Why didn't you fight harder to stay"?! The pain seems to be taking over again. Fall is here and the days grow shorter and I feel trapped in the house. The weather is still warm yet I feel chilled to the bone. Rick left me here to fend for myself. He was the only one who could lift me up out of this darkness he would allow me to be myself and feel confident while doing it.

9/25/2012 - I have felt so sad all day, tears have welled up several times, and I hurt both mentally and physically. I was driving in my car and I just start crying, I was thinking about how Rick made me laugh every day. I have nobody making me laugh or even smile much. Sure, I laugh with my sisters and Annie keeps me smiling, but in a normal day - nothing. I miss those laughs that kept me loving life.

9/29/2012 - I kept busy this week, I went to a Sox game with Patty and we had a good time, even though they lost. Went out with my sisters on Friday night, and Saturday night our whole family got together and we took Bill and Patty out for their 25th wedding anniversary. It is rare to get Billy and Sammie both to join us, good food and a good night out.

10/1/2012 – October, already the days are shorter and the nights are cold and we haven't even turned the clocks back yet. I miss Rick's warm body when I climb into bed.

I saw Dr. Tom the other night and told him about my thoughts and reasons for not eating right and not working out. He said he's always in my corner and he wants to help me realize that my health comes first. Since then I feel lighter and calmer, started working out and making healthy choices - well sort of - it will take awhile but I do feel OK about taking care of me and moving forward.

10/3/2012 - Another big change for me! Not only has my hair been cut shorter, my hairdresser convinced me to go darker. She decided it was time for change and for a new Janice. Not sure if I love it yet but this goes along with my journey of changes.

10/6/2012 - I finally got to spend the day with Amber and we hung out in the town of Geneva. It was a very interesting day from the start. The first shop we walked into, the woman started talking to me about how she loved Moon/Star jewelry, which was mine and Rick's symbol when we first met and has always been in our decor and my jewelry. As the day went on, it seemed everywhere we walked in someone went out of their way to chat with us or to show us things, example - we saw a private wine tasting room to have a party and we were told how to make use of rocks and shells, there were several other little things throughout the day. Amber said to me 'I love spending the day with you and Rick'! It did feel as if he was walking and talking with us all day. I love spending time with Amber; we get along and really enjoying ourselves with no effort, thank you Amber for being such a bright light. I felt so uplifted at the ended the day, as I drove down route 31, I talked to Rick the whole time. I remembered all the little parks along the river we had gone to, our famous canoe trip when we dumped ourselves into the Fox River and all the walks we took in St. Charles and Geneva. I did feel the tug of nostalgia but it made me smile, I felt as if he was my tour guide for the day.

10/9/2012 – I started a workout routine at the gym. They are having a "buddy" challenge and my manager Tim and I are partners. He is a good motivator; I did 29 pushups in one minute, pretty good for being out of shape! I'm feeling that good pain.

I looked for the Meteor shower but it's raining. I know they're out there somewhere streaking through the sky, I can't see them but you can – lucky you.

10/14/2012 – I helped move Cindy into Nick's Friday and Saturday then spent the rest of the weekend at the Erin's house. Annie is just about 17 months and a ball of energy; it was a great way to release the stress of all the moving.

Another strange occurrence happened, I was showing Annie a text message her mother had sent me with pictures when suddenly a picture of Rick that I took on vacation popped up. It's not even in any text message it's in my photo gallery! Just Ricky's ways of letting me know he's there with me.

Are you the air that I breathe - the sun that warms me – the Moon smiling at me?

10/15/2012 - Tim and I are in 5th place out of 18 teams at the gym! So far I'm feeling great.

I had a dream that I met a man. I was in a store and a rainbow was in front of me, looked like a card or magnet that had fallen or was drawn on the ground. I say or I hear someone say, I hope there is good fortune at the end of that rainbow. As I look up, there's a man in front of me and our eyes meet. I have no idea what he looks like, the dream ended there, I just knew we connected.

10/16/2012 – Words to a song I heard today – "even though I really love you I'm gonna smile cause I deserve to, it'll all get better in time".

10/17/2012 – I saw Quinn and we talked about putting me first. I need to stop thinking others are too busy or that their problems are bigger than mine. I'm very sensitive about what's going on in people's lives. With my sisters for example, both of them are moving and I feel as if I can't talk about my feelings, I don't want to appear insensitive to what's going on in their life. Quinn said I tend to push my feelings aside and think I'm a burden. I'm going to work on that, I went through 18 months holding back my thoughts and emotions.

10/19/2012 – My body is exhausted from all the moving, Cindy is finished and Patty & Bill are moving tomorrow. I'm sure getting a workout from all the stairs and carrying boxes.

10/23/2012

BLISS

From start to finish our life was bliss - Not one day without a hug or a kiss

We had our spats - nothing that mattered

You were my champion - you lifted me up out of the darkness

and into the light

The grief may be easing but I still feel the loss

The words "I love you" are now etched on my heart

The warmth of our love brings me comfort at night

10/25/2012 – There seems to be much talk of me moving on with my life, stop standing in my own way. My future is out there, go for it. Between Quinn and Tom, that seems to be all we talk about, just start moving forward. So as I think of what's next, what's out there for me, I wrote the following.

MY HERO

I am my guide I am my leader - My footsteps will take me where I need to be

My mind is open my heart is true - Trust in myself is all I need to do

You were my hero you were my rock - You always managed to hold me up

You were my light you were my sun - A smile from you lit the darkest corners

I'll walk alone I'll walk strong - Your hand on my back I feel you pushing me on

The time has come my future is here

With faith in myself there won't be any fear

If I start to slip by my side you'll be

I'll hear you whisper go on Bunny you're free

The thoughts and words are all there, but the action scares me to death. Afraid to fail? Fail at what? You don't even know what's out there. Is it my age, and I too old to try something new? Come on, what do you have to lose? You have the knowledge; there is nothing to hold you back except yourself. So, open the windows let in the light, walk through those doors as they open for you, who knows until you see what's on the other side. Just remember, if you had held onto your fears on May 11, 1997 you would have not met Rick.

10/27/2012 – I decided I need a couch instead of the two large recliners in the loft. The furniture in the living room is indoor outdoor to make it look like a four season room, cute but not very comfy. So off I went to shop, I found the color size and style I want, now I need to get the two recliners out. Someone came today to take one and Cindy and Nick are taking the other one. The space is empty and another part of Rick's life with me is now gone. We used to curl up in those chairs and watch TV, sometimes even sit in one together. I know it's just a chair, but the memories are there.

THE VOID

I look at the space where you used to sit

A gaping void where nothing exists

A vision of you I'll keep in my mind

It will carry me through the darkest of nights

Things come and go and can be replaced

The memories of you can only fill that space

11/4/2012 – Forty years ago I married my first husband Mike, 27 years ago tomorrow he died.

Sitting at home, thinking of all the sadness, I had a couple glasses of wine and fell asleep on my new couch, what an exciting Saturday night. Now we turn the clocks back, I don't care about the extra hour of sleep, I care it will be dark by dinner. Dark and cold are two terrible combinations, our lives get plunged into dark and the temperature drops. I love Mother Nature, but I'm not of fan of late fall.

11/10/2012 – Time passes and I feel as if I have nothing to write. Days go by and I have nonsense bits and pieces of thoughts going through my head, they move so quick I can't even grasp what the thought is. I'm not focused on the sad and lonely thoughts right now; I guess this is me moving on with my life. The empty spaces are filled with exercise, being with friends and being OK with living alone. It will be another busy weekend spending time with my sisters and then going to see Annie. She's getting more talkative and such a funny little character, we can't figure out if she calls me Auntie or Titi. She knows who I am and she runs to hug me now, just like Sammie did when she was a little girl and it melts my heart.

11/13/2012

YOUR SILHOUTTE

I walk along the beach my toes barely touched by the wash of the waves

I look ahead and see your broad bronzed shoulders

Your silhouette so familiar to me

I shield my eyes from the sun trying to make out your face

Who else could it be but you - You wave to me I pick up my pace

Waves splashing up my legs - Sun is so bright the sky is so clear

You still seem so far away - You're standing there looking out over the water

I can't see your face why won't you look my way again

I hear your voice whisper in my ear - Wake up wake up wake up

I open my eyes to a dark room

It was a dream - just a dream a sweet sad dream

11/14/2012

WEIGHT OF LONELINESS

Darkness falls all around me - I feel buried under the weight of loneliness

I surround myself with friends and family

Yet I feel so alone at the end of the day

The emptiness of the house seems too much to bear

All these months gone by I still look for you in every corner

Your presence seems so strong - I believe you're right beside me

I want to reach out and touch you

Feel your lips as they brush against my neck

A tear runs down my cheek is it mine or yours

Does your soul ache for me as I ache for you

My life journey was meant to have you always by my side

Walk with me now as I face the path ahead

11/18/2012 – I went to Allison's wedding this weekend, my first formal event on my own. Thank God the Bersani's do not allow you to ever feel alone. I had a great time, I did miss dancing with Rick, although some of his cousins did their best to fill those shoes.

11/19/2012 – I pick up the urn as I'm heading upstairs and I start to talk to you. This is the usual occurrence at least once or twice a day. Tonight went something like this – "we're going up to bed darling. I should be saying this to you instead of carrying an urn and talking to it. We should be talking about the holidays and where we're going on vacation." I set the urn down on my dresser I kiss it and continue talking. "I try to be strong honey; my words come out all strong and kick ass like I'm really that brave. I try to be brave, but I would really like to curl up and wait for my time to see you again." I start to cry and I'm stroking the urn as if it's your face. "Ricky I want to look into those eyes one more time I want to see your face and see you looking at me. Your eyes will tell me I'll be OK. I want to see you in my dreams I know you've been in some, but I don't see your face. I would give anything for you to tell me you're watching over me." I press my forehead against the urn; my tears leave streaks as they fall down the sides. I continue crying, stroking the urn and talking to you. "I want to hear you and see those beautiful eyes, but you're dead Ricky you died right in front of me and I'll never see or hear you again. As much as I wish, it will never happen. I will not wake up from this nightmare and your eyes will never look at me again. I'm here alone and I need to be brave, I pretend in my head that you're talking to me. I remember how you said I love you and I'll just keep hearing it in my head". I stood there and cried hugging the urn.

11/21/2012 – It's the night before Thanksgiving and I passed on a couple chances to go out. Cindy and Nick invited me, but I decided I did not want to make the drive there and back. A guy I've known for years wanted to go listen to a band, I originally said yes, but cancelled at the last minute. Question is - why did I cancel? I was looking forward to it, but suddenly felt uncomfortable about going out with just the two of us even though I knew it's not a date, just a friend. So, I choose to stay home alone over going out and having a fun evening, once again fear held me back. I'm just not sure what I'm afraid of….having fun?

11/22/2012 – Happy Thanksgiving! I'm thankful for the lifetime I spent with Rick. Although it was a brief moment in the span of time I cherish each day, each kiss and each I love you. I'm grateful for the life I have and the wonderful memories I carry in my heart and mind. Thank you to my family, my extended family and loving friends, without you I would truly be walking alone. For all the shoulders I leaned on and the arms that have held me up - thank you.

11/24/2012 – It's been a week filled with family and friends, really feeling the love. I'm even looking forward to decorating by house this year for the holidays. I'm planning where to put Christmas lights and even the tree. It's my holiday now, mine to plan, enjoy and spend as I want. I'll look forward, try to see the future, yet take each day as it comes. Life is mine to mold as I want; as with clay, bend and shape it to suit me.

12/1/2012 -December is upon us once again and the holiday season is in full bloom. I did decorate the house and I do not hate the tree this year.

Yesterday - I was feeling angry with God, the universe and Rick. As it happens many times I was suddenly overcome with anger and sadness. I started saying "there better be a good reason Rick's not here with me. How dare you take him from me, someone who really needed him in their life! For what - what could be the reason? Rick would love to save the children from pain and suffering, he could guide women to safety. His power of persuasion and gift of talk could bring world leaders to reach agreement. Yet I'm only hearing of war, killing and terrible things happening to women and children. I'd like to know Rick's energy is doing something good in the universe; I want to see it and hear it. Prove to me you needed him that badly that you had to take him from me. I want to know he's watching over me and keeping me safe and pushing me in the direction I need to be. Show me, prove it, I want to feel him here - I need him too!

Today - I ran some errands and was gone several hours. When I got home, as usual I said hello darling and I kissed the urn. I started to tell Rick about my day and my plans with the girls for tomorrow. I continued talking to him and suddenly I heard a sound like tinkling glass and I froze where I stood. I couldn't tell where the sound came from; I grabbed my phone and ran upstairs. A champagne glass had fallen off the shelf in the bedroom. This is the same shelf our wedding picture had fallen off when I was talking to Rick one day last year. The glass is next to that same wedding picture, and just like the frame when it fell, it did not break. I don't know how it survived the fall it's very thin glass. Hmmmm, maybe Rick is here and he just got my attention, I wish I knew what he's trying to tell me.

12/6/2012 – What is it with me and spiders?! I was sitting at the kitchen table reading the last entry I wrote in this journal. I read it out loud because it pertains to Rick and if he's trying to send me messages. As I finished reading, I closed the journal and looked up and said "so Ricky are you here, you're such a trickster". Are you trying to tell me something or just trying to get my attention"? Suddenly a spider dropped down right in front of my face as it's spinning on its web! I'm sorry I had to kill it, but it's the third or fourth time, as I'm talking out loud to Rick, a spider shows up. He knows I hate spiders and he is such a prankster. Rick, you could find another way to get my attention.

12/9/2012 - I want to move on and enjoy life yet I can't let go of the past. I cling to it like a life preserver. I try to remember everything, every detail and it gets harder and harder as time goes on. I forget some parts of our story yet some are crystal clear. I know you want me to get on with my life and be who I'm supposed to be; it still feels wrong as if I'm cheating on you. I don't want to try to enjoy life; I need it to come naturally be a smooth transition. I still feel guilty if I've enjoyed myself a little too much. And God forbid if I have thoughts of meeting someone new. I still have moments where I'm shocked into the realization Rick is dead. My mind sets itself free but my heart beats out the reminder to not forget Ricky. I could never forget him nor would I try or want to. How do I incorporate those loving wonderful memories into my new life?

12/12/2012 - They say this as a lucky date - for whom?

Sometimes I can hear myself screaming. I know it's in my mind yet I wonder if I should let it out. I was logging off the computer and Rick's picture is my wallpaper, in fact Rick's pictures are everywhere. They're in every room of the house, in my car, on my phone and my office cubicle, all filled with pictures of Rick. As I look at my screen I can hear the screaming in my head, but what good will and do. I screamed that day over and over and nothing changed it did not help or stop what was happening to Rick. Why scream now? I find myself looking at the pictures, having a fond memory, then, I hear that screaming in my head and the memory turns to sadness. I haven't cried in awhile, not really cried, my eyes well up every few days as one thought leads to another and then a few tears come.

12/13/2012 – Early morning and I just saw a meteor streak across the sky. What a beauty, it was Rick saying hello.

6:30PM - Losing a friendship is a sad event and it's like going through a divorce. Finding out just how cruel that friend can be, makes it a blessing she's no longer your friend.

12/14/2012 – Cookie baking day and we have so much fun. The best medicine is love, laughter, sisters and friends. We all went out later for pizza and met up with Debbie. All day we were blissfully unaware of the horrific killings of 20 children at school in Connecticut. Once again it puts the importance of live for today into perspective. My wish is that their souls rest in the arms of angels.

12/15/2012 – I just returned from the local dry cleaner Rick used to go to, it's been two years since they've seen him. He would go there every month, I only went once in awhile but they knew me because of Rick. They cried at the news of Rick passing and they both hugged me. This is the impact Rick had in people's lives; from best friends to the local merchants Rick definitely left his mark.

KISS GOODBYE

I can remember like it was yesterday   standing on that sunny shore

How could we know on that fateful day   it was our last kiss goodbye

The words I love you mean much more today   you're no longer by my side

148

I'll always remember on that sunny day   it was our last kiss goodbye

Pictures of your smiling face   remind me of our love

The hugs and kiss as we walked that shore   are the memories I have now

How could we know on the fateful day   it was our last kiss goodbye

our last kiss goodbye

I actually recorded this poem as a song. The melody came into my head as I was writing the words. My voice sounds terrible, by the meaning behind the words is clear.

12/16/2012 – As I'm writing out Christmas cards, yes I am sending cards this year; I wrote a letter to one of Rick's friends Marty. The following is what I wrote to him:

'I could not bring myself to send cards last year, 2011 seemed to be stuck in January for me. The holiday was very difficult to get through and nothing made sense to me. Thank God for my sisters, Rick's Cousins and all my friends. I hated Christmas, I felt as if the brightness of the season was mocking my sadness. As the year has gone by my mood has lifted and I also realize his friends and family suffered as much as I did. My loss was also their loss. The conversations you shared could never be duplicated by another. We need to share our memories. Rick always made me laugh and the stories of him still do, it's been the best remedy for healing.'

I started having this same conversation with some of the cousins. I realized I'm not the only one suffering.

12/18/2012 – I had a meltdown at the office today, nothing to do with work but my appointment with Quinn just got canceled. I start to cry and felt as if I was having an anxiety attack. The next best thing was to e-mail Cindy and text Amber. I felt stupid for losing control and they were both trying to calm me down. Amber finally called me to make sure I was OK and she told me to call Dr. Tom, so I did. Thanks Tom for listening, and talking me through a rough hour. The holidays are getting to me more than I admitted or even realized. We talked about how my grief of losing Rick might be easing but I'm grieving over the life with Rick that I also lost. My perfect, I have everything I want life. All those years of struggle, divorce, trying to find Mr. Right, were put to rest and mostly forgotten once I met Rick, and my life did become perfect. And now, missing Rick is a daily thought deep in my sub conscious and pushing itself out. The anger and grief of losing the life I had is making itself known to me and as Tom and I talked the anger became more apparent. I have to start again and I don't like it. For 15 years my only focus was our life together, it was easy; we did not have to work hard to keep our love alive. Life was simply I love you and you love me and we gladly showed each other every day. My life was set the path was paved and we didn't even need a map to follow it. Everything was shared and we took care of each other, it really was the perfect setup. We took care of the things we actually enjoyed doing nothing was a chore, well maybe the dishes, otherwise we had it made. With one tick of the clock, my world as I knew it stopped. I lost my love, my best friend, my support person and my life. So, here it is almost two years later and the grief is still fresh and raw. I feel as if we ripped open another layer.

12/23/2012 – After my midweek melt down things did calm down a bit. I finished some last minute shopping and Quinn was able to get me in for a session Saturday morning. It helped start the Christmas weekend with a fresh perspective and clearer mind. I went to Joe and Brenda for their annual Christmas party, great food and of course the famous Bersani hugs. I spent the night at their house and we stayed up late talking about their childhood. There were tears, laughter, soul cleansing and love.

12/24/2012 – Christmas Eve and I'm spending the day alone wrapping up a few presents. My morning started with a smile, I talked with Annie on the phone and she said I love you Titi and her version of Merry Christmas. As Linda and I talked I could her Annie saying hi Titi over and over, she melted my heart and I was wishing I could hold her right then and there. It's damp and dreary but my tree is lit and I'm burning candles. I'm going to head to the stores just to be out and about for awhile. This could either be long boring day or let's make the most of it day, check back later. It turned out to be an OK day; I picked up pizza, had a glass of wine and settled in to watch some TV. Now we'll see about Christmas Day.

12/25/2012 - Christmas 2012 I'm up early and I'm having coffee and getting the sweet potatoes ready for Patty and Bill. I did not go to mass so I took a few moments to pray and gather my thoughts. These are my wishes for Christmas and the New Year.

Pat and Bill finally have things going in the right direction, I ask that 2013 be a better year for them financially and health wise. Work on getting Bill in better shape for his own health, take the stress out of their lives, I'd like to see them smile again. For Billy and Sammie - keep them safe and healthy; keep them from harm both mental and physical, I wish for them all the joys in life. For Cindy and Nick - thank you for bringing happiness into their life, they are good together; keep them safe and healthy always.

Thank you for surrounding me with loving family and friends, my beautiful great niece Annie who lights up my life. My Guardian Angels, who have watched over me in my darkest hours, you kept me from despair. Mother Mary, I've asked you to give me grace and patience, thank you for your gentle guidance. I ask now to continue your guidance, your protection and show me you light. When I start to stumble, I know your gentle hands will keep me steady, and move me in the direction I need to go. Merry Christmas!

12/27/2012 – I was thinking - what if it was me that died and Rick had to go on alone? Where would he be in the stages of grief? Would he have held my pillow at night lying in my spot imagining me there? Would the tears soak his pillow as he cried himself to sleep? Would he write about me and us, and talk about us endlessly? Would he stare at our pictures, burning the images into his mind trying to remember my smile, my laugh and the sound of my voice? I think we would all like to believe life could not go on without me. Yet, we know that is not true, in fact it's almost impossible unless senseless measures are taken. Your loved one dies and the very next day life just goes on. You can stand still and watch it move around you, but really your life also is moving along. I believe Ricky would've done all of, if not more of, the things I did the past 23 months. His heart would ache, yet he'd get up and go to work, some days it would be unbearable yet somehow the next morning would come. Before you know it time has passed, so much time that you wonder what you might have missed. There are days that you were barely there walking through a haze just trying to keep your emotions in check. So many mornings you would rather hide under the covers, somehow you drag yourself out. Who else will pay the bills, clean the house and feed you? It now becomes your new way of life, you hate it at first, you're so used to sharing everything but eventually you get a routine and life goes on. The hardest part now is allowing life to move you forward.

The guilt starts to nag at me, I don't know if it's OK to laugh or have a good time. Would Ricky go to these parties and accept all these invitations to be with family and friends? I think he would want me to be me again. We used to say we were selfish with our time, it was our time and we shared it with others sparingly. We would pass on some invitations just to be together and do our own thing on the weekends. Maybe that's where the guilt comes from; I'm not passing on any opportunity to be out with other people. It's not like we did not have a social life, I met up with my sisters every other Friday night, I'd go out with the girls every month and Rick and I would host dinner parties or meet for dinners. Mostly we were together at home or planning weekends and/or day trips. It's been part of my life for 14 years to always check in before making other plans we always put each other first, it's a hard habit to break. Even though he's not here I sometimes feel as if I'm running out on him. I stop and think what would he be doing right now? As I pick out an outfit and fix my hair and makeup I wonder if he would be disappointed, expecting me to stay home forever. I wonder if he thinks "how could she have loved me so much yet she's out there having fun now?" I certainly would want him, if the roles were reversed, to meet up with his friends his personality was much too big to shut down. I know he would never forget me just as I will never forget him. The tears may lessen, the pain in my heart will ease a little bit, and Ricky will always be in my mind and heart. I need to live again and learn to get past the guilt; I have to believe Rick would want me to. It's not a matter of me forgetting Rick that will never happen; it's realizing that it is OK to go on with my life, take whatever that means and let it happen. It seems so simple just to go on yet fear is very strong and putting fear and guilt together is a superpower. This all sounds so silly when I read it back. The thought process one goes through in times of stress, trying to convince one's self it's OK to live! But it is exactly that process I need to go through. Me, and me alone have to argue with my mind and heart and come to a compromise. Convince the heart it can carry Rick forever yet the mind needs to be free of the suffering, to be rid of the guilt yet still feel the pain of loss. These are all lessons to be learned.

12/29/2012 - The first steps I need to take are to get me healthy again. Working on the mental is hard enough; I'm kicking and screaming holding myself back from a healthy physical life. I binge ate four tins of cookies in 15 days! I'm like a drug addict I'll do anything for a sugar fix. It's all out of the house now and all the crap at work is gone too. I've no excuses, just eat better and the rest will follow, I will lose weight, exercise and look and feel better. Just do it!

12/31/2012 – New Years Eve

I did not want to stay home this year so I invited myself into Nick and Cindy's plans, we went to dinner with his sister in law Chris and another couple. We changed our original dinner place to Biagio, at first I did not recognize the name and Cindy reminded me it was where we had the funeral luncheon. They do have good food there and this was going to be a fun evening, so I did not give it a second thought. We sat and I toasted to the

New Year "time for a clean slate and look forward to the new". The guy's got up to go outside and the girls were sitting and enjoying their drinks. Suddenly a waiter stops by and he asked if we were doing OK, I answered "we are pull up a chair and join us" he answered "wish I could but I have to work." Next thing I know he's right next to me saying "I would love to sit down and look at your gorgeous eyes" he then turns to Cindy and says "yes I am openly flirting with her, how could I not. I mean look at her eyes." I laugh and subconsciously or nervously cover my wedding ring. He looks and asks "are you covering your ring? Where is your husband?" I answer "he's here in spirit" and he answers back "good what are you doing Friday?" I just laugh and he grabs my hand and asks my name. I tell him and he tells me his name is Rick, I was floored. He said he had to get back to work please consider it and asks for my number. Of course the girls are all excited saying go for it, do it, beside his name being Rick he's also a bald guy with pretty eyes. The rest of our evening I really didn't see him again, he flies by our table once more gives me a look. As we're getting our check I see him looking and I signal goodbye to him, he comes over and hands me a note with his name and phone number. How ironic we ended up there and an opportunity opened for me. I'm considering calling him it's that guilt holding me back. I'm not interested in romance but it would be nice to laugh and talk with someone again, I really need to think this through. Even Cindy said the whole thing was strange as to how he ended up on our side of the restaurant, "one minute we look up and there he is talking to Jan." He was working in the same side and section where we held the funeral luncheon; she tells me Ricky sent him over.

We all went to Deb & Peters to ring in the New Year. Happy New Year and to new beginnings!

1/8/2013 – So a new chapter in my life has begun, not sure where it goes or even what it's going to be. For the first time in 16 years I've started a conversation with someone who wants to go out me. This past week I was actually a wreck, I felt sick to my stomach just thinking of calling this guy, his name is Rick and that makes it even harder. Linda and Cindy pointed out I married two Mikes, but another Rick, how can I keep from constantly comparing. I finally got the courage to call him, it was Saturday night I figured he would be working and that made it easier on me to just leave a message. He called me yesterday and we talked about an hour, and we ended with let's meet for lunch on Friday. It makes me smile and feel good to have someone interested. He said I have beautiful eyes and that I'm beautiful. He asked - don't you hear that all the time? It took all my energy not to say, I did every day from my husband, instead I answered - no not lately. Like I said, it's nice to have a man show interest and to talk and laugh with.

1/12/2013 - I still have moments where I'm overcome with sadness and fear grips my stomach. It hits me so hard and fast I swoon, almost dizzy and nauseous. A sudden burst of tears sting my eyes, then just as quickly my heart calms down and the panic passes. The memory bursts into my thoughts of Rick dying; a flash of him lying in the water then it's gone. It's been almost two years and that pain and memory is as fresh as if it was yesterday.

1/15/2013 – The two year anniversary is right around the corner. I've been feeling very anxious with a knot in my stomach, as if my body is preparing for the horror to strike again. I've been thinking about the days leading up to Rick's death. My mind seems to bring back those memories whether I want to or not, it's how I will handle them that trouble me. I will feel the sadness and remember Rick, try not to get dragged down into the darkness and despair.

I had a good talk with Dr. Tom tonight and told him about New Year's Eve and the waiter that I met. He said the whole point was not being flirted with; it was how I reacted to it all. Being in a restaurant where we had the funeral luncheon and having a guy named Rick come up to me could have gone very bad. I did not crumble or cry, yes I was freaked out when he said his name was Rick but then I laughed at it. That was the test of it all how I reacted or did not react. I came out the other side feeling good about the whole evening. I got the courage to make a phone call several days later, I felt empowered I allowed myself to be open.

1/18/2013 – Two years ago today Rick passed away. I took today off to honor him and to be with my thoughts. I woke feeling the dread of what was to come. I remember that sunny morning and our early cab ride to the Hilton hotel, passing the resorts that we would someday visit. I remember walking the beach together looking for rocks and shells, laughing, lounging, and enjoying the sun and the beauty of the water. The nightmare started sometime after 9:30 AM and he was pronounced dead at 10:30 AM. That sick feeling still hits me today; the reality and memory of Rick's death still strike that cord of fear. My tears came early today; in fact it was the middle of the night. I sat up quickly, remembering what day it was and the tears flowed for a few minutes. I said his name, I love you, I miss you, and then I hugged his pillow and fell back asleep. The rest of the day was filled with phone calls, text messages and Facebook friends wishing me well and sharing in the loss of Ricky. I spent the evening with my sisters and no more tears were shed. I miss him, I ache for him, and I'll remember that smile and the way he made me always feel saying "you're beautiful darling". I smile more about the memories and the tears have lessened but the loneliness persists.

To all of you that have been on this road with me these past two years, thank you for your support. You've been my shoulders to cry on, and the hands to steady me when I thought I could not go on. You've listened patiently even when I repeated stories of Ricky; you have to admit they are good stories. To my sisters, my family, my friends and my Bersani brothers and sisters I couldn't ask for better people in my life. We have mourned, cried and laughed together and I love you all.

1/19/2013

OUT OF THE DARKNESS

Crawling out of the darkness and quicksand of despair

finally taking a breath of fresh air

My steps slow and steady standing on my own now

Can only mean I'm ready - ready for what - the answer still unclear

As the doors open I'll step through with no fear

1/21/2013 – President Barack Obama was just sworn into his second term, it was a privilege to watch this historic and moving event. I really missed having Rick here during the elections, he was so good at interpreting and explaining the political climate. He was my political guru; he would break it all down into simple terms. All the pundits and posturing that would go on confused and drove me crazy. As many times I might have rolled my eyes as he would go on about the daily events, I'm missing that so much right now.

1/25/2013 – Two years since the day of the funeral, the last time I looked at Rick before they closed the coffin. Two days later I was going home with an urn filled with his ashes. Two years! Some days it's such a distant memory, and others I'm right back in that room. I almost forgot what day it was, I looked at my calendar and actually had to think about the date. Should I feel guilty? Or is this normal? It seems as if I go for days without those memories yet I think of Rick every morning. I still say good morning when I get up and goodbye as I walk out the door. This has become a habit now, not a teary, wistful, I can't leave the house because I'm leaving you goodbye; it's just built into my day. My thoughts are more focused on me and what my plans are. I can walk out with a cheery "goodbye darling – I'll be home later" and have no remorse that I'm gone all day or for the weekend.

1/29/2013 - I hate change! I am a creature of habit once I'm comfortable with something whether it's the route I drive or the way my furniture is laid out I will stick with it. My car is 11 years old uncomfortable with it why change? Will the past few months had been constant change. Yes, losing Rick was the biggest and heart is changing my life that I had no control over. There are changes I've decided to do for no other reason but for change. My hair not only was cut shorter, but I'm now a brunette. I moved all the furniture around on the first floor, and previously got a new couch for upstairs. These are simple easy changes that I controlled. Now, I've decided to open myself up to meeting a man. As I mentioned the guy I met on New Years, we're meeting for lunch this Friday. I'm ready to laugh again, and that's all I'm thinking about, no romance, no love….not yet. Although what happens could be out of my control!

1/30/2013 – One of Rick's buddies posted a great message: "it's just over two years since we lost our Paisano Rick. Miss you Div and I hope the water is clear and just the right temperature all the time wherever you are swimming. Salut!

2/1/2013 - Well, all this planning and worrying, my meeting with that guy fell through. I was actually relieved I was a nervous wreck all day. Not nervous to meet up with him, more about the expectations he had, I'm just looking for a friend and I wasn't sure what he was looking for. Just stressing about this for a few days it already feels like it's too much work to start a new relationship.

2/3/2013 - I'm letting go of all the sorrow I hung onto, now what? For two years my life has been defined as a widow, and prior to that I was Rick's wife. I clung to that sorrow like a life raft; it was the only way of life I've known. It allowed me to move through my days unseen and mostly unnoticed. I had strong fortified walls protecting me from the world. The minute I stepped outside those walls I was seen, life rushed in on me. It will swallow me whole if I can't stand on my own two feet and I'm just learning to walk without crutches. I've opened the door and there's no closing it.

2/10/2013

I've been making plans for my trip to Cancun in April. I'm trying to track down Olga, who worked at the Hilton and was such a big help the two days of planning to get Rick home. Memories are flooding back. I want to go to the beaches we loved and scatter some of his ashes. I would like to go back to the beach where he died and have my own memorial for him. With all the memories of the two days, that first night alone was the worst. I don't think I wrote much about it. I didn't start writing until a few months had passed. This is what came from those memories today.

THE MOONLIT NIGHT

Moonlight streaming across my face waking me from a beautiful dream

Sleepy eyes gaze out on the starlit night the sound of the ocean so serene

Screams rise from the back of my throat the beauty of the night lost in horror

I search the room you're nowhere in sight

you've left me here to face this alone

What nightmare is this that has replaced my dream

The beauty of the night is not what it seems

I ask the universe what cruel trick have you played

I yell at the moon and stars to please go away

My true love is gone - I'm wearing his shirt his scent still lingers

The middle of the night the truth sets in - never will I gaze at his face again

Scared and lonely I hug myself tight

Crying I call out his name all through the night

How could you leave me why didn't you fight

Morning comes and I face the day - The start of the rest of my life

Without you beside me - without being your wife

2/11/2013 – I've decided 2013 is my year of discovery. I had the year of loss and pain then the realization year, now it's about finding me. Discovering what's out there for me and who I am.

2/14/2013 - It's Valentine's Day I miss my Big Dog.

VALENTINE

Valentine Day   Lovers unite

Promises broken   Bleeding Hearts cry tonight - They weep in vain

2/27/2013 – The past couple of weeks have been quiet, both mentally and physically, I started walking again and I feel good. I never heard from waiter Rick again, deep down I'm both relieved and yet wondering why he abruptly changed his mind. At one point the familiar feelings of "I must have done something wrong" popped into my head, but I shook that off quick. It was a brief encounter that showed me there is a life out there for me. Now, I'm open to the idea and ready for my next encounter.

My thoughts have not been focused on anything in particular, the days fly by and the weekends are still difficult. I try to keep busy but Saturday nights seem to go on forever. I need to stay positive and focus on my health. Keeping fit and strong is my goal now. Moving forward, carrying my memories with me and looking to make new ones.

2/28/2013 – The t-shirt, I still wear it the scent of Rick long gone. Some nights I still wake up calling out his name.

3/2/2013 – First weekend in March and we're covered in snow, starting to get cabin fever. I need to get outside; walking in the cold does not interest me. I better start doing something; I'm in a bathing suit in four weeks!

3/4/2013 - Ricky come to me in my dreams. Tell me secrets. Say you Love me. Let me know I'll be ok.

3/10/2013 – I had a full weekend with my sisters and spent a couple days at Erin's. I'm blessed with such wonderful sisters and family. The euphoric emotional high leaves a smile on my face and a light in my heart. Driving home as I'm near my exit tears well up realizing again my home is empty and quiet, and nobody to share this feeling with.

3/12/2013 - I have so much going on right now. I have an appointment with a financial planner to get me on track for retirement and budget my money. Quinn and Amber think I should start a support group; maybe I could have meetings at Dr. Toms. Amber sees me reading excerpts from my book, getting it published and having music written from my poems. They have such faith in me; I need a little help from my friends. I love that they believe in me, it's scary and a bit overwhelming. A new life is being offered to me I needed to step up and take it.

Rick - stand by my side, soothe my fears and doubts, allow me to see my strength and make the right choices. Many paths have been laid at my feet; guide me in the correct direction. You have always been my champion and my sounding board, now it's all my choice, I must believe in me as you did. You are watching over me and you surrounded me with wonderful people to lean on and help me. I feel you by my side and I can hear you cheering me on "Bunny my Darling, you are a strong fierce goddess have no fear".

3/18/2013 – The world is pushing in on me, I feel like giving up and hiding. I don't know how Rick juggled all the responsibilities. I'm trying to get my finances in order, deal with the rentals, go to the office and work without all these distractions clogging my brain. It's not in my DNA to handle legal and money issues, I get overwhelmed and I want to shut down. My eating goes crazy and my health sufferers. I'm angry that I inherited these rental units; it's not as easy as one would think. The association has rules and so does Elgin, too much paperwork and dollar after dollar being spent on licenses, filings and repairs. Then, the thought of not having enough money to live on weighs heavy on me. I always loved going to work, it keeps my mind sharp and meeting and talking to people is always a perk. Knowing I HAVE to support myself, has turned that to a grudgingly dreary task. Rick sheltered me from all the involvement with the rental units; he did it to protect me. Now in the light of stark brightness I'm blinded by my ignorance. I'm getting too old for this! I should be planning a fun retirement in a few years, not trying to make ends meet.

3/31/2013 – I've been busy with work and picking up last minute items for my trip. It's Easter Sunday and I woke up feeling run down, I wore myself out from stress so I'm staying home today. I'm missing out on a Bersani get together but I need to rest up I leave next Saturday. I'm going to Cancun, back to where Rick died. I have mixed emotions; I'm excited and nervous, wondering how I'll feel as I step off the plane. As the sights and smells hit me, how will I react? I have no expectations; I will take each moment as it comes. We'll have a memorial at Playa Secreto and I'll scatter ashes there. I'm sure staying at the Grand Mayan will bring back a flood of good memories. I don't want to over think the trip, just let each moment have whatever impact it brings. Gloria and Brenda will be my support when I need it.

4/1/2013 – Monday, and it hit me in one swift punch, I'm leaving in five days for Cancun. That nervous, sick feeling crept in and keeps thumping my heart to remind me it's there. Hello! Where have you been? I've been tanning, buying travel items and laying out my clothes. You just connected mind and body and realized we we're going. Don't freak out, don't panic, it's OK to be nervous; it is a big deal going back there. Just try to remember all the good memories too. Ugh! The more I tell you to calm down the faster my heart beats. I'm feeling that same fear as the morning I woke up alone. How can I face this? The answer is with the strength you've gotten through the past two years. Let the fear come, accept it and let it wash over you, and as in your darkest hours it will pass. Cry if the tears come, face the pain; allow the memories to flood in. The worst that will happen is remembering it all over again, that is the point of this trip, facing those memories.

4/6/2013 – The day is here it's 5:30AM and I've been up since 4:30! After days of nervous energy I'm anxiously awaiting our group to get ready.

4/7/2013 - It's our first morning at the Grand Mayan, yesterday was so full I did not have time to think. As soon as we got to our room we put on our suits and went straight to the pool bar. I jumped into the pool, after a little coaxing, had a drink and some much needed food. Later we took a long walk down the beach, got our bearings of the resort and then back to the room to get ready for dinner. All my fears of having an emotional breakdown were swept away. All the good and funny memories of Rick were shared throughout the day. It's a new day and I woke up in paradise; take this as a symbol for your life, all is not lost. There is love and beauty in life and it is mine to enjoy, do not squander this opportunity of life.

We're thinking of ways to have a memorial at the beach, Brenda and Gloria are really on board and coming up with sweet ideas. As we went off for a morning walk, we talked about how we wanted to send Rick's ashes into the water. As we turned the corner I saw the perfect vessel, it looked like the outer skin of coconut shaped like a bowl. Brenda picked different colored flowers and I found some shells and rocks. I sprinkled a bit of ashes and we arranged the rocks, shells and flowers into our vessel. The three of us walked out onto the rocky beach, I got brave and kept going and we ended up chest deep in water. We had scouted out this spot earlier making our way through the rock and coral. With my fear of water I could not believe how far I had ventured out. The water was so calm after the windy wavy day yesterday; I think Mother Nature knew I needed to be out here. As I stood there the waves gently rocked me and I was overcome with the feeling Rick was right there with me. I got so relaxed in the water I actually let the waves lift me and float me around, it almost felt as if I was being lifted and carried in the water. I felt the peace wash over me and tears came to my eyes. I could hear him telling me how proud he was that I had walked into the deeper water. When we went back out there with the ashes later we laughed all the way and I no longer had the fear of being in deeper water. We prayed and said the Our Father; I then said a few words sending him off into the waves. As I released our little boat it bobbed along and then started heading back to shore. We were laughing and Gloria walked out further and finally let it go, it floated for a bit than a wave turned it over as we watched it float away. We had carried my camera out there and took some pictures; this is another beautiful memory that will be with me the rest of my life. I could not have imagined how peaceful this moment would be. When we came back to shore a woman asked if we had just done a memorial. She had just lost her husband in November; we sat and talked for awhile and later met up with them after dinner. She had been married 35 years and he also died in a tragic way. I could see the fear and anger as she talked and she asked how I had gotten through. We compared the pain we were going through and I told her how I write and talk to a therapist. I believe we were meant to meet each other. I hope she took away that missing him never goes away; yet your life will be filled with laughter again. We all stayed up much too late and drank a little too much but we laughed the whole time and it was a very healing day.

4/11/2013 – The last few days have been relaxing, good food and great conversations all in a beautiful tropical setting. Not only is my body being nourished by the sun and warm air, so is my soul. Brenda and Gloria have been the best medicine for healing, lots of talking and laughter.

We walked the beach to Playa Secreto, this was a favorite spot of Rick and I. It was a very windy day and the surf looked rough and I picked a spot to scatter Rick's ashes into the water. *"Ricky may your spirit forever ride the waves*

164

of life." As we stood and watched the waves roll and crash I could imagine Rick jumping and body surfing. The image quickly changed to the day he died, I could see him fall over as the waves carried him in. The tears came as the memory of that day rushed back, I cried as the sadness came over me and turned to hug the girls. We stood there together for awhile; just watching the waves and remembering. The sadness passed and we talked about the days Rick and I spent at this beach. Such wonderful memories I have that will also be with me forever.

I stood and let the waves wash over my feet and I gathered energy from the water and I could feel Rick all around me. As I turned to walk away, once again a wave came and smacked me in the butt, Rick's way of saying hi Bunny. We spent the rest of the day lounging by the pool and talking about Rick, love and life.

After dinner we walked down to the pool area where they held a little market. I stopped dead in my tracks as I heard the music from the speakers playing La Melaguena; which was a song we heard in Mazatlan. Rick would ask for it to be played everywhere we went. It's an unusual song and very difficult to sing as the notes are very high. I had just mentioned it to the girls the night before at dinner in that exact same place. There was a strolling trio and I had said I should ask them to play it but I never did. I looked for the girls so they could hear it, as I came around the corner one of the vendors looked at me and said listen to the beautiful song. He then sang a couple seconds of it and I was shocked that he would point it out to me. By the time I found Brenda and Gloria, the song had stopped playing. The vendor looked at me again and tells me he studies music, so I jokingly said "why don't you sing it?" He answers no it is a very difficult song to sing, I agree and we say how beautiful it is and I start to walk away. He suddenly pulls out a guitar and proceeds to sing the whole song to me, I know Rick was with me and made sure I heard that song. I sat by the pool and let the tears come as I remembered those memories of Rick in Mazatlan and our other trips to Mexico.

4/12/2013 – Our last full day and I took a walk along the beach, stopping to watch the waves and take in the feel and the sound of the water. As I walked the same path I did with Rick; I imagine him by my side reaching to hold my hand as we would walk along checking out all the rocks and shells. I did find a rock shaped like a heart it will join the collection at home.

THE MONSTER

I stand at the water's edge facing the monster I feared

Wash over me now bring me your strength

Surge through me let me feel your power

Wash over me now I fear no longer

I will take your power my feet firmly planted

Standing strong I welcome you - Wash over me now I feel your caress

Gently you rock me as my fear pours away

A monster no more my love holds me tight

Surround me now as you carry me - My tears fill you

My spirit breaks free - I face you now as you wash over me

4/13/2013 – Brenda and I took one last walk, we went down to the beach and stood silent, lost in our thoughts. We said goodbye to Rick, took one last look at the water and left to get our bags.

As I got into the taxi I had tears in my eyes and I had that fear hit me once again. At the Airport I became agitated and nervous and the memories flooded my mind of my last trip home from here. My heart was pounding and I found it hard to catch my breath. I took a walk to calm myself it felt like I was leaving Ricky there again. After my walk I focused on the wonderful trip we just had. A piece of Rick will always be here and I carry him home in my heart.

4/14/2013 –UGH! Back home to cold weather! I'll try to remember the sights and sounds of Mexico and the feel of the sun. Today is Patty's birthday - off to her house for cake.

4/15/2013 – Another senseless act of violence; bombs went off at the finish line of the Boston marathon. Over one hundred injured and three are dead as of now. A horrific moment once again showing how precious every day is and how life can end in a second. Don't get caught up in the planning for tomorrow that you forget to enjoy today.

4/21/2013 – It's my first full day alone in 2 weeks, I miss all the conversation and laughter. Yet it is nice to have some quiet time, but the days do drag without the interaction. It's too cold to spend any time outdoors, can't wait for some sun and warmth. I'm spending the weekend with Linda and Annie, oh how she'll light up my heart.

4/24/2013 – I've been thinking back to my week in Cancun; the sights and smells that I feared so much actually comforted me. As I stepped into that warm, breezy air I felt at ease. As the sun warmed my skin, the air embraced me and I could feel Rick all around me. I was home, the anticipation I felt was not from fear after all, I knew I was coming back to Ricky. Every familiar step I took I knew Rick was right beside me; I even slept a deep peaceful sleep. I was not coming to say goodbye, I was rejoining Rick and saying hello to my love. As we rode in the cab back to the Airport; my heart was heavy as I was saying goodbye once again. Then I realized I'll be OK, that I have him all around me. My heart and mind carry him always. The next time I go to the ocean, I'll know Rick's spirit is where he loved most, riding the waves and he'll be there waiting for me to return. And as the sun, ocean breeze and water caress me - so shall he.

4/26/2013 - Spring is finally showing its face, the grass and trees are getting greener and the sun feels warmer. Wonderful! The downside for me - my Spring/Summer clothes do not fit.

5/8/2013 – I started walking every day and I'm trying to eat better, I see some progress and my clothes fit a little better. I'm walking two 5ks soon, I know it's not a marathon, but it's a good start for me.

5/11/2013 – Happy Birthday Annie! She is two years old, time is flying by. She is a true light in my heart and the purity of her love is such a gift. She lifts my spirit with her laugh and hi Titi. As I stated before, she is a gift from the angels, in my darkest hours came this beautiful glimmer of light and love leaving me no choice but to open my heart and let her in. I took one look at her precious little face and I knew I was given a new purpose in life. Thank you God for the direction you guided me to and continue to light my way and show me my path.

5/12/2013 – Happy Anniversary My Love. This is the third time this day has arrived without you here. Today I smile at the memories of that day: The beautiful weather Mother Nature bestowed on us, the way you looked at me as I walked down the aisle to join you, the way we stared into each others eyes as we said our vows, how happy and giddy we were in the limo ride to the hall, our entrance to Simply The Best, your beautiful speech, singing to you as we danced our first dance, the smile on your face all night long and how many times we said I love you. I remember all that and our wonderful 10 years of marriage; I remember it all today with a smile.

I'm spending the afternoon with all the Bersani's to celebrate a christening. Twelve years ago we all partied at our wedding; it was a beautiful way to spend the day with them today.

No tears shed this year although a few times I did well up. I'm focusing on all the good loving memories and they bring a smile to my face.

5/15/2013 – I walked a 5k today in less than forty five minutes, it felt great. I'm doing it again Saturday. I don't want to get too cocky, I just started!

DID YOU CRY

Did you cry as you left me as I cried for you

Were you scared as you left me as I was scared too

Were you at my side as I knelt over you

As I kissed you goodbye were you kissing me too

As I cried through the night were you holding me tight

When I'm sad and alone do you wish you were here

And on the days I feel stronger do you send out a cheer

I'd like to think all that is true I live my days in memory of you

You taught me well on how to handle life

One of the many perks of being your wife

As the days lead me farther away from my heart you'll never stray

Your belief in me is what gets me through my days

As the grief lessens and I'm finding my way

The memory of your smile will light up my day

5/16/2013

DARKNESS

Darkness a cold shroud that surrounds me

unseeing   unhearing   buried deep

Darkness a comfort that blankets me   protects me   shields me   hides me

Darkness an anchor that weighs me down

shackles me   binds me   restrains me

Darkness leave me now   free me   allow me to move

to see   to feel   to hear   to live

I look to the light to lift me up   blind me with your Glory   your beauty

I break free of this bondage   I walk alone   I walk tall

My eyes see the wonders of life

I hear the song birds   I feel the warmth of the sun   alive yes I will live

I will live   yes I am alive

5/19/2013 – I walked another 5k yesterday and a couple miles today, just keep moving, feeling good, looking good and eating right and stay on track.

I booked my next trip to Cabo at the Rose for next January. I'm going whether anyone else comes with me or not, brave talk I know, yet I think I can do it.

5/20/2013 - I saw Quinn tonight, I started this journey with him two years ago, and I've come so far and have gotten much stronger. There are still those moments that hit me in the gut, and just for a moment I forget Ricky died. I'll have a memory flash through my brain, and one minute I'm smiling and in a split second my heart breaks again. The effect does not last long these days; it just hits and then passes quickly. We talked about me getting out there and meeting someone, yes dating, just start slow make a new friend and put myself out there to try new things. I could sign up for online dating, but the ideal way would be someone I know introduces me to someone they know. I have to let this brew in my brain for a while, in the meantime I smile and say hello to a lot of men.

5/27/2013 – Well, I did it! I signed onto an online dating service. Two years, four months, and nine day since Rick died. Am I ready? Who knows! I won't know until something actually comes up. One funny thing, right after I completed the profile and uploaded a picture I got a few looks and some comments, two were in their twenties and it gave me a good laugh. I guess you can say I've opened the door let's see who enters.

How often have I said I miss your hugs, your kisses and hearing you say I'm beautiful? I've missed those everyday and I've longed for them and cried over the loss of them. I had a conversation with someone from the dating site, if you could call it that. Right from the start all he talked about was hugging touching and kissing me. I kept interrupting saying that we were on different pages and I finally just ended the call. I realized not just any hugs or kisses will do, I miss yours. I might be ready to start a new friendship; but the thought of any physical contact makes me shudder both from fear and disgust. After I hung up I got angry and I started to cry. Ricky, if you had not died I would not be going through this B S! The bar is set high as are my expectations; I may be alone for the rest of my life. Ricky, if there is someone out there for me; please guide us toward the same path.

Quinn asked me if I was a strong woman and do I think I could stand up for myself in uncomfortable situations. If this first conversation is any indication as to what I need to filter through, I did not come out with a very good rating on myself. At first I laughed when he asked me if I was into younger guys and I changed the subject. I laughed again, when he responded to my next question by asking "do you sleep nude?" I said "tell me about you" and again he came out with uncalled for comments. I finally got angry when he asked how long I'd been single and if I had been dating. When I told him it was over two years his response was that I must not have had sex in that time and he could take care of that for me. I said it was disrespectful and he just didn't get that losing a spouse is so different than divorce. "I'm not out to party and get crazy" I said. "Too bad" was his answer "I could work on changing your mind". UGH! Hopefully this is not the normal, I'd rather stay single.

6/10/2013

THE WISH

A young girl innocent and pure always wondered what would become of her

As she sat and stared out at the sky on the perfect star she made a wish

Someday bring me a love - someone kind and gentle to hold my hand forever

Together we'll walk through life and wonder at the world around us

We'll walk along the waters' edge and love the greens of nature

Through many rises of the sun and golden glow of the

Moon we'll watch as stars shoot by

The taste of love had touched her life but not the lasting kind

As the days and years flew by

so she thought did her time to find that magic love

She wondered if her days would end always wishing on a star

I thought I'd find a special love that kind and gentle man

He'd hold my hand forever and we'd walk through life together

We'd walk along the waters' edge and love the greens of nature

With every rising of the sun and golden glow of the Moon we'd watch as stars shoot by

One bright and sunny day her wish was finally granted

About the time she'd given up in walked the man she wanted

A smile that would brighten each day and eyes filled with love

This gentle man swept into her life and quickly stole her heart

Days together they would spend and talk about the future

It was then she realized how her prayers had all been answered

He told her he'd been wishing for the same thing all his life

172

I'll be a kind and gentle man and hold your hand forever

Let's wonder at the world around us and walk through life together

I'll take you to the watery shores and walk the paths of nature

Through every rising of the sun and setting of the Moon we'll watch as stars shoot by

So on bended knee he took her hand and asked please be my wife

In their years together each day was filled with bliss

Not one day would start or finish without a hug and a kiss

As they walked together her hand he always held

Many sandy shores and paths of green in their lives they did behold

Never taking life for granted - saying I love you every day

How her heart was broken the day he was taken away

Now their story has ended but only here on earth

For every path she walks and every sandy shore

She knows he walks beside her with his hand holding hers

Every morning with the rising sun to the setting of the Moon

She stares out into the open skies wondering how it all ended so soon

And upon each star she places a wish someday once again she'll feel his kiss

As her life continues thankful she'll always be

For the time they had together and her wish that was granted

In her heart she'll carry the memories that were made

The gentle man that held her hand and loved her everyday

Shared her love of nature and walks along the shore

The splendor of the universe and all it had in store

And as a shooting star lights the night sky she'll always believe it's him saying hi

6/16/2013 – This is the end of the second journal this had some of my toughest and most heartbreaking moments. As I come upon 2 1/2 years of Rick's passing; I'm now starting a new journey. I've ventured out into the world to be seen and heard by others, others meaning men. This will be a tough journey, I'm at a crossroad, my fork in the road, however you want to say it, and I'm at a crucial decision point. I keep saying I want to meet someone and move on with my life. How do I start making new memories when old memories still bring me to tears? As of today I have been in contact with four men. We've been emailing each other and at some point, maybe, meeting one or more of them is going to happen. As my new journal begins; so does my new journey. I will still continue to write my feelings of loss as they come up. This will now be the story of a new life and my new adventures. Not just meeting men, but Jan in the world discovering more and more each day. My sadness was a safe haven hid from the world; I'm stepping out from under it. Wish me luck and good fortune.

6/30/2013 – Just when I think I can face another day, and feel OK about being alone, the onslaught of tears hits again. I signed up for a dating service and I was being all brave about meeting someone new. Once I started getting messages from men the fear and uncertainty set in again. I don't know why but I still feel as if I'm cheating on Rick. I need to be open to start any type of new relationship; it would not be fair to any man if my heart was not open to letting him in. I've been keeping everything welled up in my brain as I have not written in a couple of weeks and it's starting to drive me a little crazy. I need to remember to put my thoughts down on paper as the familiar signs of self doubt and guilt start to add up. I'm eating sweets, basically overheating, lying around and not working out, I'm feeling sorry for myself but not doing anything to change it. Just when I think I have my strength up to full force I knock myself down again. I feel as if I'm so desperate to meet someone, because I am so lonely and bored, I'll leave myself vulnerable and easily taken advantage of.

7/3/2013 - It's 4th of July weekend already, at least I'll spend time with my family and the Bersani's.

7/5/2013 -I met one of Rick's school buddies Randy who now lives in San Francisco, we contacted each other through Face Book. He was in town for a school reunion and we met up for the afternoon. We shared stories, mine were of the wonderful, funny, loving husband that Rick was and his were of the mischievous actions of youth. I find it so easy to carry on a conversation with a total stranger as long as we talk about Ricky. We laughed, there were tears and we laughed again. We talked about Rick's love of California and his desire to go back to San Francisco. I gave Randy a small container with some of Rick's ashes asking him to scatter them in some of Rick's favorite places and we talked about me coming out to visit him to do the same. A couple days later he told me he had put the container of ashes into a zip lock baggie and went swimming in the hotel pool. He asked if I thought he was crazy, but I laughed and told him the idea was brilliant as Rick loved to swim. He said it was the best swim and most laps he had swam in a long time, just as Rick was with me in the water in Cancun I believe he was helping Randy swim too.

7/8/2013 – I took a long walk in west Dundee into Carpentersville today. This is the path I walked many times with Rick and then alone in the past year. I have many memories of holding hands, clear crisp days and watching Rick kayak.

I saw two hawks flying high above the river and thought of us

As we soared through life together unaware of the world below us

High above the fray and nonsense of life suddenly one flies alone

175

7/13/2013

IMAGE

His image permanently burned into my brain

his voice constantly whispering in my ear

When I close my eyes I still see his smile

I know I feel his arms around me as I sleep

I'll carry him with me for all time

in my heart and my mind his love will continue on

7/17/2013 – I ask you Ricky, my guardian angels and supreme power of the universe; please lift this burden from me, I have endured over two years of loss, sadness and loneliness. You must think I'm some superpower and I can handle as much as you can throw at me, but at some point I will break. I'm asking for help to sell the Rental Property as I've taken on enough this year and the past two years. Please remove this stress from my life.

Randy and I were messaging each other and he wrote "moving on does not mean leaving Ricky behind". I was shocked and surprised, I had written that statement months ago and it is hanging on my refrigerator. He laughed and said "wow I thought I made that up, do you think Rick is sending messages through me"? I said I wouldn't doubt it; Ricky always gets messages to me somehow. I told him, now that he has some of the ashes and if he talks to Rick, to watch for signs and messages that Rick might send his way.

7/18/2013 - I'm fearful of moving in any direction or making a commitment to my life. I say I'm bored and lonely yet I'm afraid to open the doors in front of me, opportunities are there I'm just afraid to see them. I swear this is exactly where I was last Summer I've been stuck in neutral for a year! Get moving! No need to run or even sprint, just get one foot in front of the other and walk the path before you know it you'll travel miles.

7/31/2013 – It's the end of July already. I'm still waiting for that first connection on the dating site. Had emails from a few but no meetings yet. Once I meet the first man, on any kind of date, it will become more natural for me.

8/8/2013 – August already…I don't even remember July. Annie is getting so big and smart; she's talking up a storm and has such a personality, I really need to see her more often. I went to see Blake Shelton with Cindy and Debbie, my first Country concert and of course it was a good time with those two. I finally got an offer and sold the rental unit. That stress has really been weighing me down; I ended up sick having to take a couple days off work. Don't even get me started on the dating site! Thought I was going to meet someone, never heard from him again. Then another man said, yes I'd like to meet for coffee, asked for my phone number and never called me. After couple weeks I emailed him and he answered back that he's second guessing being on the dating site and he's really not ready. Too bad he seemed very nice and he was a widower too… I give up.

I wonder if there could ever be anyone else out there for me. Do I really want to give my heart to anyone? Am I just going through the motions, yet keeping my mind and heart closed? Perhaps that's why the opportunity has not arisen, negative thoughts lead to negative actions, just saying.

8/16/2013 – Happy 23rd Birthday Sammie! I walked the Elvis 5k last night with Cindy and Debbie; this year we walked through Lincoln Park. After that we decided to keep on walking, heading back to Debbie's we found a fun bar serving $5.00 martinis. It was a good way to spend the rest of the evening after a long walk.

I took today off and Cindy and I decided we didn't walking enough last night so we headed down to the lake to do it again. We ended up around Montrose beach and we walked until we found a lovely nature area, there I scattered some of Rick's ashes. As I scattered the ashes into the water I said "here you go Ricky back to the lake you loved so much" and Cindy took pictures to capture the moment.

8/19/2013 – Well, I signed a contract with actual matchmakers, don't ask me how much it costs let's just say I could go on a great vacation with the amount I spent. The real positive, is that everyone that signs with them are screened and are of the same mindset that we all want to find a match. The girls said I should be getting a call shortly with my first match; this is truly making a commitment.

8/26/2013 - I spent a few days in St. Louis visiting Linda. We always have a wonderful time together we shopped, went to the show, hung out in the pool, relaxed and we walked every day we even walked a 5k. Early Saturday morning I had a very interesting experience. Her husband John is the athletic director at Washington University and he had us come out and ride along with the trainers for the rowing team. It was a sunny calm morning; we spent about 2 hours on the water watching the teams train. Truly a new experience for me to spend that much time on a small boat rowing around a lake, it was lovely.

8/31/2013 – I got a call from the matchmakers and they're setting me up with my first match, his name is Dennis. He call this afternoon and we talked about an hour and we're planning on meeting this coming week. He was charming and funny but a little dry, he has a sailboat and loves to bike, two things not in my wheelhouse but let's give it a try. One thing to note; I was not nervous at all talking to him or setting up the date. This is a big change from six months ago; I'm really looking forward to meeting and talking to new people and eventually dating seriously.

9/1/2012 - Cindy and Nick have booked the hall for their wedding - August 30, 2014! The theme will be tropical and the ceremony and will be held in the gazebo overlooking the golf course. Did I mention she asked me to officiate? I get to be a reverend! I'm so honored to perform the ceremony for them.

9/5/2013 – The unofficial end of summer already, time really slips by these days. I have my first date tonight; we're meeting for drinks at a restaurant and I'm feeling very calm. I do not have any expectations details will follow.

The evening went well for my first date he is very nice and attractive but a little boring. Our differences became obvious as the night went on, he is very much into his bike riding and boating. He was easy to talk with but there was no connection or attraction, which is actually a good thing I did not fall for the first man I met. I did think it was weird to sit for 3 hours at a bar, have two drinks, and he never offered food not even an appetizer. Bottom line I went on a date! It felt normal, OK, and the right thing to do for me right now. I got two hugs and evening of conversation and now I'm ready for the next time.

9/11/2013 -12 years ago the World Trade Center came crashing down after the two planes hit them; how our world has changed since then. I was remembering how everyone pulled together after that; there was such a bonding and feeling of brotherhood, it seemed compassion and patience was normal. It did not take long for the ugly and mistrust to rise up again. Here we are on the verge of stepping up against Syria; the civil wars will be part of our lives forever.

9/12/2013 – I just booked a flight to California to visit Randy in San Francisco. I'll bring ashes with me and we'll go around to some of Rick's favorite places, of course the Golden Gate Bridge, and scatter them in the place he truly loved. It was a last minute decision and I'll be staying at Randy's, I know we just met but I trust him like a brother already. I'm seizing the moment because they past too quickly.

9/14/2013

CHASING STARS

You could think of life as a scratch off ticket - just a roll of the dice

Don't even think twice - just take what's next around the corner

Save yourself a dollar and keep on walking

You can stand in line play follow the leader and do what you're told or

Make yourself heard and break the mold

Take life in your own hands and be who you are

You're not on the outside - they just can't see that far

It's the fools that don't get you - it's their loss you see

To miss out on the ride as you chase the stars

I followed in line I did what I was told

I couldn't run I was under control - Nowhere to hide life had its hold

Now you can't hold me down - step by step I'm gonna take this town

Step by step I'm gonna set me free for all the world to see

Keep walking to your own beat - no need for directions or to get any clues

Just set your rhythm and hit the streets - there's really nothing to lose

Keep your head held high go out on your own

Walk that parade called life and keep beating your drum

As they sit on the sidelines and watch you go by

You're original no need to explain

As you keep to your truth - they'll see who you are

180

You've got nothing to prove and everything to gain

The world is yours just keep chasing those stars

I followed in line I did what I was told

I couldn't run I was under control - Nowhere to hide life had its hold

Now you can't hold me down - step by step I'm gonna take this town

Step by step I'm gonna set me free for all the world to see

Rock and roll cool or blues - it's your song even if it's in your head

Sing what you hear - dance like you don't care - there are no rules

Smile at their backs when they turn away

You know where you're going - the ones that matter will always be there

I followed in line I did what I was told

I couldn't run I was under control - Nowhere to hide life had its hold

Now you can't hold me down - step by step I'm gonna take this town

Step by step I'm gonna set me free for all the world to see

9/26/2013 – I've turned to food for comfort and companionship. I pour my heart out to a bowl of buttery popcorn, I have quick chats at the counter with spoonfuls of ice cream, and I ponder the crisis in the world with sweet potato chips. Pictures of you are scattered all through the house; how I long for the days of hugs and laughter. You're gone and I face every day alone. I've gotten used to waking in an empty house it's the nights and weekends that boredom sets in. The TV is another companion, too much so. I treat it like a friend; I talk back to the programs and try to change the outcome. I reason with the criminals, cry with the bachelorette and I take sides with the housewives. I need more in my life, at least on weekends; I know boredom is not a reason to date; it's just part of it. You and I shared everything and I miss that the most; all the conversations about anything and everything. I know I said this was my year, well its September I have not made a change or much of an impact in my life. It is time to set some goals and put them into action.

9/30/2013 - Even at the office I feel alone, I get isolated from conversations by my ex friend. We do not speak at all unless it relates to work, and that does not happen very often. The tension is unbearable some days. I know we'll never be friends again I could never trust her. It would just be easier to chat like work buddies, a simple hello would make life easy but we can barely be in the same room together. A 20 year friendship ended that quickly and now I feel as if we have nothing in common. But this too is a loss; she was a close friend and now even at the office I have no one to talk with. I won't trust anyone else, everyone is just a gossip and there's no need for the whole office to know my thoughts. The sad thing is I go for days with bottled up emotions and thoughts I need to share with someone. This is why writing has helped me so much. I don't get to spend enough time with my other friends or my family and I don't want to burden them with such heavy thoughts and sadness. I miss seeing Amber on a regular basis, too much time passes between visits. Life and distance have made it harder to meet up.

10/8/2013 – I just got back from San Francisco, I took the offer from Randy to stay with him for a few days. We tried to get in as much sightseeing as possible and went to some special places to scatter Rick's ashes, which was the reason I came. We took a ride into Marin County through a beautiful area called Nicasio, we had lunch then headed to the Golden Gate Bridge. It was a beautiful clear day, we walked to the center of the bridge and at sunset I scattered some ashes out into the bay, "let your soul and spirit fly over the city you loved". We ended the night walking around Fisherman's Wharf and scattered more ashes at the beach belonging to the swim club, which we thought was so appropriate for Rick. The next day we walked around Haight Ashbury, I could imagine Ricky back in the 70's with long hair and hippie glasses walking the same streets.

After a long day of walking in and out of t-shirt and head shops and great people watching, we headed for Ocean Beach for the final destination to scatter more of Rick's ashes in San Francisco. It was a stunning night, a slight chill in the air and red/purple sky with bonfires burning up and down the long stretch of beach. I walked to the waters' edge imaging Rick by my side as I watched the sun set. I sprinkled his ashes into the gentle lapping waves, my final goodbye to Ricky in San Francisco. His spirit is all around me now and my mission here is complete. I longed for him to be at my side, holding my hand and pulling me close to keep me warm. I stood alone, a solitary figure at the waters' edge as the Sun set and darkness surrounded me. The scattering of Rick's ashes was bittersweet; he always said he would come back here, never thought it would be like this.

11/9/2013 – I can't believe the Holidays are right around the corner again! This year has gone so quickly, I hardly remember Spring or Fall. I've been staying busy this past month going out with my sisters and friends and trying to see Annie as much as possible. Erin is expecting a baby boy in May and I'll have another baby to spoil. I also won $500 from a radio station, which was pretty exciting.

The tension at my office is very high and it's difficult to know who to talk to as sides are being taken. I have not discussed the breakup of my friendship with anyone in the office; they only know we are not speaking to each other. I've cut myself off from most of the group just to make my days easier, but it leaves me so alone now and some think I'm just being anti social. I'm still trying to survive and recover from the loss of Rick; I don't need this additional stress of grammar school behavior.

11/14/2013 – I need to open myself up to see the light, to allow the light to come into me and guide me. I need to open myself to allow those that I'm supposed to meet, young and old, to help me write the next chapters of my book. Right now my book is nothing but blank pages. Finding the right path to walk is fairly easy, going out and trail blazing your own path and being your own person is a real life challenge. Going forward can be scary; but being alone the rest of your life is downright frightening.

11/27/2013 – I'm afraid to give my heart to someone and have a broken. And I'm more afraid to have it shattered again from a loss, not because I couldn't handle it, I can't think of mourning for anyone else but Rick. I struggle enough with meeting men for a drink; I tell myself it's not betraying Rick, but giving my heart completely to someone else seems like the ultimate betrayal. No matter how many times I hear "it's what Rick would want" is it? How do we know for sure? What if his soul has the same pain and loss as mine? Maybe he cannot bear to see me with someone else. As I write this I know it's not rational thinking. I wonder - if my heart and soul ache and break into a thousand pieces who knows what we can feel on the other side. My love and caring for Rick is so strong I couldn't think of hurting or betraying him. This is my hurdle now; I think this is the toughest and highest one to handle. I still carry the guilt that if I move forward I leave Rick behind as just a memory.

11/28/2013 – It's Thanksgiving, I miss Rick everyday and long for him, but today is about giving thanks. Everyday I'm thankful for the years and life I had with Rick. I'm thankful for the home we shared and all the love and laughs we enjoyed. I give thanks for my family and friends who have loved and supported me. I'm thankful for each day I can move forward and honor Rick with how I can carry on with my life.

Bring peace and serenity into my life let my light shine so bright to gather those near me that are to be with me and shine so bright to blind the evil and negativity around me.

12/1/2013 – I put up the Christmas tree today hoping to bring cheer and light into my house to lift my spirits and open my heart.

I miss Rick so much that I put the cologne samples that come in the magazines into Rick's bathroom so every time I walk in and catch a whiff of the scent it reminds me of him and makes me smile.

12/14/2013 - Ricky are you disappointed in me? Did you think I'd be doing more with my life?

12/15/2013 - The power of prayer and positive thinking have shown itself. I've been asking about my new path and the people I should be meeting and in walks a woman Daniela, full of life and funny as hell. We met and it's as if she's a long lost sister, so much positive energy is around her. She is a singer and asked me to go to a charity event with her I'll be meeting a whole new group of people. Ask and ye shall receive.

12/24/2013 – The last 10 days have been filled with babysitting Annie, the annual Bersani Christmas party, and a party at my neighbors tonight. My eyes fill with tears as I'm reminded of the emptiness and loneliness that is now my life. After all the fun and laughter the silence of the house and the absence of Rick still scream out loud as I walk through the door.

12/25/2013 – Merry Christmas 2013. All is well with my family as we come to the end of 2013. Patty & Bill are doing better and getting back on track. Sammie is almost finished with college and will graduate in May and Billy is doing very well at his job and I'm filled with pride for both of them. Cindy and Nick are planning their wedding for next August. As I look back on the year, I'm doing well also. I have great friends and family; I'm making new friends and looking forward to what's next.

1/1/2014 – Happy New Year! Gloria and Dean had a New Year party and it was a wonderful evening. We told great stories and there was lots of laughter throughout the night. Peace and happiness follow me every day.

1/7/2014 –Carrie's husband died and the wake was today, she is Rick's cousin. They were married 52 years; he's been the only man in her life. She looked so lost and fragile. When I went up to talk to her she said "oh someone who can understand what I'm going through". I made her promise to let us all in to support her.

1/10/2014 – As I sit back and look at 2013, which by the way passed too quickly, I realize the year was uneventful. By that I mean, not much is going on in my life actually it's been boring. Yes I meet up with my sisters every Friday and I'll meet Amber for lunch once in awhile, but I'm boring. I've had a few great trips but I have no hobby or interests. Who is Jan and what does she do? I thought 2013 would be the year of discovery for me - I was wrong. Unless discovery means I've settled into my life and I'm OK being home doing nothing but relaxing. I need to define who I am before I meet someone to date. I cannot be defined by who I am with, my life needs to take a turn and have some direction. Some days I just want to be alone and do nothing and some days I'll look to do just about anything. I'm not going to force it or fake it; life as I know it will go on as is for now. The thing is I'm good with that and I like me.

I've heard that eagles nest along the river in the Winter, as I was taking a drive into Geneva I started looking for them. As I approached Route 31 I started talking to Rick about wanting to see the eagles. I pulled over by the river but none were to be found. But as I continued over the bridge I saw two eagles sitting on a branch and again further down route 31and I saw two more by the park where Rick and I had rented a canoe. I continued talking to Rick about the memories I have from the park and the two eagles fly across the river up into the tree. I'm so excited I almost gave up my shopping trip but I knew I would be heading back this way. I went back to the bridge and found the perfect spot to park and started looking for the two I saw first to take some pictures. One took off and circled right over me and I got a great picture of it. I kept talking to Rick saying thank you - thank you for showing them to me and suddenly four more fly over and all six are now perched in the tree next to me. At this point I burst into tears at the sheer beauty of them in flight. I stood there crying and talking to Rick about what a beautiful thing it was and just kept saying thank you over and over, what a magical experience it was. I continued watching and it started to snow, I stood there until I was freezing and finally pulled myself away. By the time I got home I was emotionally spent. Ricky sends me the greatest gifts, all I had to do was ask and he answered. Proof he's here with me and still making me happy!

1/14/2014 - I wake with a solid steady thumping of my heart, my stomach takes a flip, and my mind reels back three years, in four days Ricky will die. My body unconsciously slips into grief mode, I sit up and sigh this is going to be a long week. My mood settles into that dark brooding place as I automatically start recalling the events of that week. It was our first day in Cancun and we went exploring, as the morning goes on I replay each moment, this will go on each day until the 18th.

1/18/2014- The days are filled with my memories of our trip; all I keep thinking is Ricky you die tomorrow. I've sat each morning and let the memories wash over me; our long walks, sunny days and how much fun we had together. I tell Rick every day how much I miss him, my heart feels heavy today. Three years ago I watched my love lose his life; yet somehow I know he's here with me watching over and guiding me. When I'm sad and lonely I can feel his comfort. When a smile comes to my face I know it's something he whispered in my ear. Today as in the past two years I remember and honor him.

HOW LONG

Has it been that long? I measure time in years now - How can that be?

Was it not yesterday I saw the love in your eyes

as you turned to smile back at me

Life continues on yet, stands still in my heart

You're with me every day each moment – every hour

You guide me from above and by my side you'll always stay

And each night as I gaze up at the stars right before I head to bed

I say goodnight my darling and as they twinkle back at me

I smile and now I can rest my head

1/19/2014 – I did something well out of my comfort zone last night as I did something for me, I went to the WINGS charity event with Daniela. This is a charity Rick and I always supported, it's a cause close to Rick's heart. He always stood to protect women and children and I know he's pleased that I attended this function. As we arrived early; I wandered around to look at some of the auction items and met up with Miriam for a drink. As soon as we sat down the entertainer for the cocktail hour started to play the piano. I heard him start to sing Into the Mystic by Van Morrison, Rick's favorite song and I also had it played at his funeral. I froze for a moment then I smiled, it was a message from Rick letting me know he was there and I believe he was pleased I was there also. When do you ever hear that song played for a cocktail hour?! I'm very glad I went, it was a beautiful event the speeches were moving and music was fun. It was a beautiful way to honor Rick this night.

1/25/2014 – 3 years ago I said my final goodbye to Rick as they carried his coffin out, today I'm headed to Cabo with Brenda. I have mixed emotions it's a much needed vacation and it was Rick and my favorite spot. This year if feels right to take care of me, I'm leaving Chicago Winter behind, its sunny and 80 degrees in Cabo and I deserve the break.

1/27/201 -I did something today I thought I would never do, get in a small boat in open water to whale watch. The staff was very informative and we got up close and personal with the Sea Lions. I thought I would be more afraid but somehow I felt very safe as we sped out into the open waters to look for the whales. We're in front of Sunset Beach and we stopped to get a good look around. I took advantage of the moment as I took out some ashes, leaned over the side and let the ashes go into the water. I told Ricky to swim with the whales and I set his spirit free overlooking our favorite Sunset Beach. I told him I was excited to see whales and please send some our way and within minutes the whale surfaced in front of us and as he dove we got a great shot of his tail. I squealed with delight, after that we saw several surface and then two came up and breached. Tears came to my eyes at the beauty and the thought of Ricky and his spirit out there with them; it was such a great day.

2/1/2014 – The rest of the trip was filled with relaxing by the pool and ocean, happy hour drinks and an afternoon massage. We took a trip into San Jose Del Cabo and our first stop was at the old church. Rick and I were here on our honeymoon. Brenda and I said a prayer and I scattered some ashes by a tree in the courtyard.

We also went to the Sunset Beach resort so I could once again scatter ashes there. Brenda had a great idea of making a rock alter on the beach and I knew the perfect spot. Down the beach is the Pedregal where all the big homes sit overlooking the water and one of the hillsides has a very large collection of rocks. Ricky had climbed onto and sat among those rocks as he sorted which one to bring home and I have a picture of him sitting up there. Brenda and I found the perfect spot close to where I had taken the picture. We gathered different shapes and colors of rocks to pile up and we made a small sign that said "for you Ricky because you rock". I scattered ashes over the rocks took some pictures and then we took the sign so we would not litter, we'll remember and Rick knows it was for him. Just knowing Rick has become part of nature in the places we loved best brings me peace and joy.

2/18/2014 – The memory of the warm sun and sand is far behind me, in fact I got so sick I went to the Urgent care with a terrible cough. I have not been this sick in 3 years! UGH I long for warmth.

3/1/2014 – I got great news and bad news today. Good news, my ex friend is leaving our department and moving to a different floor. The stress is literally walking out the door. The bad news, we'll be short handed and need to hire and train someone again. That's ok; I'll be stress free from attitude.

3/11/2014 – I've been on a few "dates" over the past couple of months, nothing special and no attraction or connection. I did meet a very nice man, a little too old for me. Not so much old in age, just his state of mind and his health. He is very sweet and generous; he took me to several Hawks games, bought me a jersey and even treated my family to a game. I had to tell him I was not feeling the same about him as he was to me. He did not believe me and he wanted to take me to dinner and more games, I finally had to say I could not see him again. It's sad, as he would have been a great friend, not just for the Hawks games, he was funny and easy to talk with.

3/21/2014 – It's a big day today, I've been with Great American 20 years today and I'm leaving for South Carolina later with my cousin Dennis and Assunta. The girls decorated my desk for my 20th anniversary; it was a fun morning now I'm in the car on the way to my cousin Nancy and Ron's. They live just outside of Hilton Head in a Dell Webb community, looking forward to the week.

3/25/2014 – It's been a fun busy week so far. We went to Savannah and we covered a lot of territory, it's a lovely city filled with lots of history. Every few blocks there's a square we sat at several of them watched a street performer and relaxed in the sunshine. We visited the Cathedral of St. John the Baptist built in the late 1700's and walked through the old cemetery. We walked the river walk and ended at a historic restaurant the Pirates Cove. I forgot to bring Rick's ashes here; it's a reason for me to come back someday. We went to Hilton Head, I scattered ashes at Coligny Beach and in Sea Pines where I climbed the lighthouse. There is a memorial for Charles Fraser the founder of Sea Pines; it has a small stage built around it and a very large Liberty Oak tree in the center of it that was saved by Mr. Fraser and I scattered Rick's ashes under that tree. We ended the day at the Chart House; had drinks and appetizers as the sun set over the river. I watched a single Dolphin make his way just off the small marina - hello Ricky. We went to a small historic town called Beaufort we walked through some shops and ended at a coffee shop overlooking the water, I scattered Rick's ashes into the saltwater river. We walked through Beaufort National Cemetery which has both Confederate and Federal graves.

3/27/2014 - The week is coming to its end, we did more sightseeing and shopping in Bluffton where they have a street fair. I found Bride and Groom Angels made from oyster shells which I had to buy for Cindy's Beach Themed wedding.

We went to Hunting Beach; a very rugged large beach area where the turtles come to lay their eggs. The beach was large and flat and easy to walk on with lots of rocks and shells also large trees lying on their sides. I loved the feel of this beach and I scattered some ashes there, I found a few small rocks and shells to take home. When we got home, Dennis had gathered some rocks and gave one to me it was shaped like a heart. Rick and I seemed to always find rocks over the years shaped like hearts, once again a hello from Ricky.

There was an old authentic lighthouse here and I decided to climb the 10 stories. I went alone as no one else had an interest in climbing and I got past my fear of heights even though the staircase was an open wrought iron design. It was a beautiful view from the top I'm glad I made the climb I could see for miles standing out on the lookout. It was a great trip with wonderful company.

3/28/2014 – Happy Birthday Ricky! We head home today back to the cold and snow.

4/14/2014 – Happy 60th Birthday Patty!! Welcome to the 60 club. We celebrated Friday and met Sammie and Billy for drinks.

4/20/2014 – Easter Sunday a time to reflect and take a look at my life. Am I living to my full potential and if not what's next? I've thought of all the love and support I've had these past three years. If it wasn't for family and friends I would have crumbled. Between my family, the Bersani's and all my wonderful friends all those hugs have kept me safe and sound. The love of all of them has filled some of the gaping hole in my heart and I love and appreciate them all. I was inspired to write the following poem for them.

HOMAGE TO THE HUG

You enter the world and take a breath

your mother's arms are your first caress

When you can't sleep through the night there are arms to hold you tight

Through tears of joy or sorrow a hug is sure to follow

In this worlds fast pace there's always time for a warm embrace

And when you think you just can't take it

a hug confirms that you can make it

Family and friends are always there they're sure to know you need some care

Arms open wide they gather you in

and hug you with love that never will end

You'll never find a more powerful drug

than the healing power of a wonderful hug

5/12/2014 – Happy Anniversary my Darling! You gave me the best years of yourself and made mine simply the best!

Erin was induced Friday night and Theodore John was born Saturday the 10th. I went to see Annie yesterday for her 3rd Birthday and Linda and I took her to see Teddy, she's in love with him already. Sammie graduates today, I'm so proud of her being the first in our family to graduate college.

Samantha the Graduate

It took more years and a few schools to finish

Detours and all you still stayed strong

I'm sure there were times you want to quit - With plenty of encouragement you really stuck with it

You studied days and nights just to get through it

Between work and school and minimal sleep

Those Red Bull drinks helped keep you awake

You even managed to get good grades

As they called your name the 12th day of May

Your family, feeling so proud wanted to scream Sammie out loud

With diploma in hand as you walked off the stage

Our hearts filled with pride

It's official now - well done you are a graduate

6/30/2014 – I spent a girl's weekend in Memphis with Cindy & Debbie. We had a blast at the bars and restaurants on Beale Street and of course we went to Graceland. I was very impressed with Graceland, yes it is a big tourist attraction but it is lovely and well kept. Walking through seeing the history of Elvis was so interesting, we spent 5 hours there. I scattered some ashes next to the angels overlooking Elvis' grave, the pool and landscaping are beautiful. Such a fun trip with those two!

7/16/2014 – Happy Birthday to me! I'm 63, how can that be?? I feel Rick all around me today.

7/19/2014 – Rick's nephew Anthony is getting married today, I'm going for Rick since he was the only uncle they knew. The ceremony is at St. Paul of the Cross; the same church where we held Rick's funeral. This will be bittersweet, a happy occasion yet filled with memories of Rick and the last time I walked into that church.

My heart races as I walk through the church doors; it's just over three years since the funeral but it all comes flooding back in an instant. I stand in the vestibule for a moment taking it all in. I see Kitty glowing with the proud mother look and I'm now in the moment of why I'm here. As I sit and wait for the wedding ceremony to begin my thoughts start to drift back again and I feel anxious and ready to cry. Kitty's brother reaches over and takes my hand, my emotions must show on my face, and with a gentle squeeze he smiles and asks - how am I doing. I give him a weak smile back and say I'll be OK. We're at a part of the mass where we remember those that have passed. Alexander and Arthur read Rick's name and tears come to my eyes and I see Armond put his head down to cry. All of his family has now passed he alone represents the Dinverno's. His two sons will carry on his name but right now I can feel his pain of being alone. My tears fall freely; missing Rick so much knowing how proud he would be of Anthony.

It's a beautiful day and the reception was held at the Park Ridge Country Club. I'm seated at the family table with Armond and Kitty and Kitty's family. As soon as the music started Armond pulled me to the dance floor and for the rest of the night that's where I remained. I danced with all the kids and the aunts and uncles. Anthony danced with me later, and with tears in his eyes said how great it was that I was there and he knew Zio was here with us. It was a fun night and I'm so glad I went.

8/2/2014 – Cindy, Debbie and I spent the evening at Navy Pier, we ate, walked around; I scattered some ashes off the end of the pier and we stayed for the fireworks. We walked back along the Lake Front to the Drake Hotel, where Rick and I were engaged. I scattered ashes in the garden area in front of the Drake.

8/30/2014 – After all the preparations and me writing the wedding ceremony, the day has arrived. I think I'm more nervous than Cindy & Nick; I want to get through the ceremony without crying. The rehearsal dinner was last night and with all the fun we had this is going to be a great wedding party.

It was a beautiful day, Cindy and Nick looked wonderful and the ceremony went off perfectly. I was nervous before I walked out with Nick but he started the crowd cheering as we walked together and that calmed me down. It was a fun reception and we all danced the night away, even Nick. I'm so happy for them both!

9/20/2014 – I'm thinking I would like to start a support group; I'd like to make it a safe comfortable setting to share feelings. I feel I can help them sort through the feelings as I know what it's like to feel lost and alone. You don't want to be a burden to your family and friends so your emotions can stay locked inside of you for too long. I would like to give them a place to release; I just need to reach out and not fear rejection. If someone is not ready or not interested I need to remember someone else will be. This isn't about me anyway so I can't take it personally, it's sharing my knowledge. It will bring a new purpose into my life; I want to work on me and my goals for the future.

9/30/2014 – I started writing a blog, thought I'd try that first. The one thing about loss is your mind holds onto feelings that your conscious mind doesn't realize are there. For me writing a journal and now a blog has been a great outlet. The first thing I wrote about was losing my Dad, which surprised me:

"My memories are of him enjoying life, sports and family. He loved the White Sox and that's who we love. He would go to the parks to watch the softball leagues and we would go with. He took us to Sox games and the Blackhawks over shadowed the night I got engaged to my first husband. I had to wait for a break in the action to tell him the news. That was my dad, and I loved him as he was. I was denied the chance to know him in my adult years, as were my sisters. All the things he missed and we missed him being there for. This was my first real loss and a long time of healing followed. This shaped my thinking; live for today and really enjoy the life you have. Don't live for your job, it just pays the bills. You pay yourself with living life."

It's been 41 years since his death, 17 since my Mom passed, 29 years since Mike died and almost 4 years since Rick died and the memories and pain still surface.

11/30/2014 – The past couple months have been uneventful, and the Holidays are upon us again. I can't believe it's the 4th Holiday season without Rick. I'm thankful for the wonderful memories of Rick and the life we shared. I have a beautiful home, wonderful family, friends and extended family and I still feel his love in my soul. I'm so fortunate for all in my life, I had two Thanksgiving dinners one with Nick's family and also went to Erin's. Spending time with Annie and Teddy kept me busy all day and my heart is melting from loving them both.

I put up my Christmas tree and some decorations around the house. Compared to how much I hated that tree in 2011 I enjoyed decorating it and look forward to seeing it lit. My heart still misses Rick but the tree now makes me smile. I have all the silly ornaments we bought together and the few he surprised me with and each one has our spirit of love. I can see the beauty in life again just as I can see the beauty in the lights of Christmas reaching into my dark corners.

12/12/2014 - I went back and read my journal to see where I was mentally, I was surrounded by sadness and darkness, feeling walled in, never seeing any light. The magnitude of how my life was affected seemed much too large to break through. I think back and some of those emotions and thoughts are now hard to remember. Thinking then, I would never truly smile, be happy or believe in life again. How did I survive it all? I was barely making it through some of those days, walking through life like a zombie. Now, my smile and laugh are true. I look forward to social events and can even handle being home, alone, with me. It's been about four years and I've survived with great strength and dignity. Many times I just wanted to quit, curl up in bed, cry and stay there forever, remembering Rick and the day he died. I managed to gather strength, from deep in my soul, and move step by step to the next day and then the next and so on and so on. Here I am today, still missing Rick, but planning ahead for My Days.

12/25/2014 – Merry Christmas! As I sip my coffee sitting in front of the Christmas tree; I remember past Christmases. Rick and I would read our cards to each other out loud sipping coffee and enjoying the morning. We would have silly gifts for each other, mostly small items that we needed for our vacations. We would relax, talk about packing and profess our love to each other. As I sit here the quiet of the house still bothers me. Even in the quietest moments I always knew Rick was in the house. The shuffle of his slippers, the roll of the wheels and the squeak of his office chair would break the silence enough to know he was here. If he thought I was sleeping too late he would stand in the doorway and clear his throat just enough to break through my sleep. He would always wait to make coffee, but that too would be a signal for me to get up. The fresh brewed aroma would seep into my brain as a wakeup call. I loved the way his face would light up as I came downstairs. "My Bunny is up"! - followed with – "I'm sorry did I wake you"? I'm smiling at these memories and my heart feels full. I miss him so much especially around the holidays and today I feel blessed to have and remember these wonderful memories.

Christmas is not about the amount of the gift, but the gift of the precious time we'll spend together.

1/2/2015 – Happy New Year! I went to dinner with Cindy & Nick and a group of his friends.

I say 2015 is the year of no excuses; I walked a 5k today along the river in Elgin. It was eerily quiet; no people just me and my thoughts.

1/17/2015 – I started looking at pictures of Rick and I and the tears flowed. It's midnight and I'm still sitting here in the dark, I need to get to bed. Of course my mind is remembering how excited we were to face the adventures of the next day heading to Cancun.

1/18/2015 - Whether I consciously think about what today is, my heart and soul will. My tears were shed last night as I poured over all of our pictures and vacation videos. I put together some of my favorite moments and created a movie online with the song The Best as the background, as our life was simply the best. Today my mind replays every moment of the morning Rick died as it has in the last four years. It starts remembering little fragments of the first four days of that trip. It's like a movie you've seen over and over; you know every line in every scene yet you need to let it play through to the end. Tears came again this morning as I watched the little movie I posted and my heart breaks all over again looking at that smile and those eyes. I miss him so much; four years have passed but there are those moments it feels so raw and new.

I love you Darling keep watching over me. After four years of suffering and not taking care of me, I'm now starting to live the words - moving forward does not mean I'm leaving Rick behind. I'm just taking care of me!

1/19/2015 - I again woke in the middle of the night, my heart racing and I was filled with the terror of being alone. When I woke up this morning tears filled my eyes just as they did four years ago. I went through the day very quiet and solemn; not wanting to talk to anyone. I think of Rick every day several times a day; yet this week the thoughts are heavier and a constant sadness surrounds me. It's been the same for the past four years. I'll allow my thoughts to only focus on those few days we had in Cancun and the horror of the week that followed. I pull the memories from the recess of my mind and allow them to be front and center. I close my eyes to remember the look of the beach and the sky. In an instant it all floods back; the smile, that kiss, I love you, the wave, the collapse, the people surrounding Rick, my screams and finally Rick lying alone covered by towels. And so it will play out the next six days until the final time I say goodbye at the funeral. Each day I will recall what I was doing, feeling and saying. For 358 days I smile laugh and enjoying life; but for the seven days from January 18th through the 25th I want to cling to the memories of those days.

1/25/2015 - Each day this week I brought back the memory of what I was doing four years ago, preparing for the wake and funeral. Today would be the day of the funeral; the last time I looked at Rick's face kissed him and rubbed his chest, it was my last goodbye. I took just a moment to remember how I felt; no tears just to acknowledge the date and time. I'm much more at peace these days. I will always miss him and talk to him every day. I'm looking forward and planning my future, my new path.

1/29/2015 – I do not need anyone to make me whole. I do not need a man in my life to make me complete. I need to make me complete, me healthy and me whole.

1/31/2015 -Brenda and I are heading for Mexico again back to Cancun. I'm truly excited for this trip, of course I wish it was me and Rick but I will enjoy every minute.

2/7/2015 - It was a wonderful week filled with lots of adventures and relaxation. We spent a day in Playa Del Carmen, found a sweet church and left some of ricks ashes there. We went to the new Cirque De Solei where we had wonderful food and great martinis. We had lots of laughs met sweet people and recharged. I put Ricky's ashes in a flower again and set it afloat into the water in front of the Grand Mayan resort. I feel so refreshed with a different mindset from this trip. I feel alive and ready to take on the world. There was no sadness and no tears on the trip; in fact I think Ricky made us laugh the whole time with silly adventures and the sights and sounds of Mexico. I come home carrying the memory of the sound of the ocean and the feel of the sunshine.

3/19/2015 – It's been a great month since my vacation. I've spent plenty of time with Annie and Teddy, Cindy retired and we celebrated that, I put my other rental on the market and have a contract. I got a promotion and a raise, there's a sigh of relief to make a little more money. Today I just won concert tickets for 5 different Country concerts!

3/20/2015 – It seems each time I talk about moving forward and starting a new exciting life the bravado soon fades and I go running like the scared little Bunny I am. When I was out with the girls we had that conversation; and I kept saying I'm ready to start my life although I'm not sure exactly what that will be. Once I have time and my brain thinks about it, I retreat. I know I'm ready; I feel it but the fear of the unknown is holding me back. I've been typing out this journal and reading it is like having therapy. There have been moments I had forgotten and moments that reopened the wounds. At the same time it's been cathartic and I feeling like I'm healing in the process.

If you fill your life with happy memories there is no room for regret.

3/28/2015 -Happy Birthday Ricky! Today you would have on 60! My darling Rick, I'm sending you kisses and love, may the Angels be singing a joyous song for you. My love belongs to you always. We would have celebrated with friends and family somewhere or maybe here at the house. 60 is a big deal we would've had so much fun celebrating.

5/12/2015 – 18 years ago my life took a wonderful turn. I belonged to a dating service back then and I was given Rick's name and phone number. I was told I would like him and the rest is history. We had our first phone conversation and talked again a few more days. Our first date was May 17, 1997 and we fell in love that night

Happy Anniversary Darling! This is the fifth time I'm saying it to an empty house and kissing an urn. Today there were no tears no sadness keeping me home I'm filled with happy memories.

It's strange not being surrounded by the sadness and feelings of endless loss. I feel as if a piece of me is missing that there is something I should be doing. I carried that sadness for four years; to let go of that weight feels like I've left something behind. Every day I get up and go through the day and I feel OK about me and my life. There have not been tears and my heart does not ache or feel broken. I think of and talk to Rick every morning and every night asking him to keep watch over me, but that deep pain is gone. Should I still feel it? That's the hardest part for me; to realize I'm not feeling guilty for letting go of that pain. I guess I'm finally crawling out of the deep dark hole into the light. I'm going to follow that light to see where it takes me. I think about how my life has changed over the past four years. I have things I do, places that I go and I spend time with people much more than I did when Rick was here. If he was here today I would be doing a fraction of these things and seeing less people because my life would be shared with Rick instead. I've been given an opportunity to start fresh to start new. I have a wonderful family and friends and I've been adopted into the Bersani family. I have Annie and Teddy to spend endless time with and be filled with joy. Yet when I come home I still feel so alone. I enjoy what I'm doing in those moments and who I am spending it with; but for some reason I don't carry the joy home with me. I admit there are still some things I need to work to on.

I was sitting at my desk thinking about Rick and wondering why I'm not sad or crying today. Three songs in a row played on the radio that reminded me of Rick. When the Cranberries song Dream came on I lost it. I sat there staring at his picture remembering how he always played that song for me. With tears in my eyes and now a heavy heart I miss him so much. I was afraid I was forgetting about missing him; but the mind plays tricks. You become so used to your 'New Normal' you somehow forgot how you got here, yet I no longer need to put on that backpack of pain and carry it around.

5/25/2015 – It's Memorial Day and I'll end my story here. I really have come so far and continue to work on me. Over the past year, I've been on quite a few "dates", I'm weeding out what I know I don't want, no extreme sports, no single obsessions (boats, motorcycles') being asked "so, you're a widow how's that working for you"? or told "you cannot wear a life jacket on my boat in front of my friends!" and "I just can't compete with a widow's memories" yet I have no idea what I do want. I think I was testing myself, just to see how it felt and my reactions in different situations. To be honest, it was for the wrong reasons. I was bored and looking for something to do, to fill up my days to make my life complete. I discovered over this journey, that I make my life complete and it's up to me to be happy with that first. Yes, meeting a nice, funny, and caring man would be wonderful in the future; I would like to share my life with someone eventually. For now, I will continue to be myself, be spontaneous, be happy, and trust my intuition and when the time is right, I'm going to just let it happen organically - as they say. The moment I truly open my mind and set my soul free to the Universe I'll be ready for the next chapters in my life to be written. In the meantime, I've learned to love myself again and realize the strength and power I have over my life. Ricky always told me I was a warrior, a goddess and I finally believe it. To move forward with strength and conviction, to follow the path I'm paving, is the best way to honor Rick's memory. He'll be by my side, cheering me on and so proud of his Bunny.

As I go forward in my life, my mind, my heart and soul are ready for what's out there waiting for me. My soul is thirsty; it's been starved for four years.

My kiss goodbye to Rick as I scatter his ashes in Cabo San Lucas

The "new me" with Ricky watching over me – 2015

6/15/215 - Just as I was bringing my story to an end and looking to publish my book, tragedy has hit our family again. June 10 about 9:30 PM my sister's husband Bill passed away at the young age of 50. I had missed two phone calls from Sammie and finally Cindy got a hold of me crying and telling me that Bill had died. I felt so helpless that I couldn't be there for my sister Patty. They had told me to stay home I was too emotional to drive that far. I was hysterical and I could not believe what I had just heard, this tragedy could not be hitting our family again. The next several days were like reliving my nightmare all over again with the planning of another funeral. But this time it was different, it was not my husband I was not doing the planning I was only there for moral support. I can only hope with what I've learned over the past four years I can be there for my sister, for Sammie and Billy.

I wrote a eulogy for Bill - I had to for Patty, the kids, Bills family and especially for Bill

Bill, Big Bill, Babe he was called   A twinkle in his eye and quick to tease

but he always knew how to make you feel at ease

A big voice with a gentle soul

Not one place you could walk where he wasn't well known

His family came first of that you can be sure

He loved his kids and was always so proud

he could almost embarrass them when he bragged out loud

When anyone needed help he was first in line

never worried about giving up his time

But that was Bill always willing to lend a hand

With a passion for sports he trained his kids well

Both Billy and Sammie carry that gene

whether watching or playing it's always about a team.

He started them young and influenced many

coaching and teaching his patience ran deep

just wanted those kids never saying defeat

Big Bill I'll miss you   your wacky humor   your big heart

and our wonderful Christmas dinners

So Babe - it's not goodbye it's only farewell for now

I know you're here with us and we'll try to be strong and make you proud.

6/27/2015 – The Past couple of weeks I've spent talking with and listening to Patty about any struggles she's having. This particular day I just felt so sad for her and all the widows that have endured these sad, lonely, painful, tiring days of survival. I can only listen and let her know I understand, I wish I could do more. I was so moved by her and reminded of my own struggles that I wrote the following poem.

I hope in reading this some comfort will be given in knowing you're not alone in this.

The Widow

She cries alone just sitting at home

People stop by or reach out by phone

She is the newest member of a private club

This group has many but each one is on their own

Not one has a asked to join it's a part of life

And the certainty of being a wife

A broken heart and endless tears

Are now her dues the rest of her life

If one should meet another a soft smile and nod they'll share

Silently saying it's OK and please take care

You see she's a widow her husband now gone

All she can think is how will I ever go on

The calls will stop and friends won't know what to say

Their lives will move on yet hers remains the same

She has to continue taking it day by day

She'll find her strength and carry on

The memory of their love will keep her strong

45325142R00124

Made in the USA
Middletown, DE
30 June 2017